UNSINKABLE

The incredible true story
of a young boy's journey
following his dream to America

A Memoir of Vincent "Winnie" Nirich

Written by Terry Gray

This book is a memoir, written from Winnie Nirich's oral recounting of events in his life. As such, it is based on his memory and perspective. Every effort has been made to make the story as accurate as possible, and facts that could be verified through reliable sources were. All stories are true, although some non-critical details and names have been omitted or slightly changed to respect the privacy of those involved.

Cover design by Vincent "Vinnie" Nirich, Jr.
Background Image © Rudall30 | Dreamstime.com

Dedicated with love to Winnie Nirich,

and all other survivors who,

despite hardships, adversities, and atrocities,

never gave up

CONTENTS

ACKNOWLEDGMENTS

To God be the glory!

He's been nudging me for a few years to write this book, but as I'm unfortunately too often apt to ignore God's little nudges, He gave me a big old shove this past summer when I saw Winnie at our annual family reunion. For years, I've said that someone needs to write his story down. Well, I guess that Someone is ME!

When I asked my husband Kim what he thought about the idea one Sunday morning in July 2014, he looked at me and said, "I think you should go for it." Thank you, Kim, for your encouragement and support. You've been my greatest cheerleader in all my endeavors these past 34 years of our marriage, and I love you with all my heart and I thank God every day for bringing you into my life!

That very afternoon I asked Judy, Winnie's wife, whether they might be interested in having me do such a thing. Her quick response, "You are an answer to prayer!" solidified that this was what I needed to spend the next several weeks of my life doing. Thank you, Judy, for your confidence in me, your smiles of encouragement, and your weekly double-doses of hugs!

Thanks to Kristoffer and Dana, Emily and Zach, Kamaron and Anique, and Kyler and Kara, my children and their spouses, for your love and words of encouragement. I think they've come to expect the unexpected from their mother since they've flown out of our nest. You all are my inspiration as you are absolutely the best accomplishments I will ever have in my life. I love all of you so much! And, of course, my six precious grandchildren, Karter, Kaden, Kassie, Kelsey, Krew, and Abram...you melt my heart and light up my life! Your Gramaw Terry adores you!!!

Mama and Dad, I can never thank you enough nor repay you for the wonderful childhood you gave me. My sisters Barb and Maria and my brother Mark, you all shaped me into the person God created me to be. I love you all so much!

Thank you to my dearest friends, Peggy and Brenda, for putting up with me and excusing me too often for missing our weekly coffee time to make time for my writing. Thanks to my wonderful friend, my spiritual leader, and my pastor/"boss" CJ for allowing me such flexible work hours to accommodate my unpredictable schedule, and for his sweet wife Leann for her excitement about this project and constant encouraging words. Thank you to Janet, my first BSF teacher so many years ago and still a very dear friend and mentor, who pushes me out of my comfort zone when I need pushing. God has blessed me richly with amazing friends!

To Donna, who at the very beginning of this journey assured me that I could indeed do this and pointed me to CreateSpace, thank you! You'll never know how much those first words made me believe that publishing a book was really doable. Thank you, Beth, for graciously taking your limited, precious free time away from teaching to proofread for me. Your positive comments were a huge boost!

Vincie, thank you for designing the cover and patiently making my vision a reality. I hope you will forgive my nit-picking and "aggressively encouraging" ways...guess it's just the mother in me! Vincie, Angie, and Gary...thank you for the privilege of sharing your dad with me and for the positive words you have given me along the way. I am blessed to call you my cousins!

But this all wouldn't even be possible if Winnie hadn't come into our family and made us all fall in love with him right from the start. Thank you, Winnie, for always having time for us kids, listening to our stories and telling us yours, and for taking us on unforgettable adventures. Our great cave adventure with my cousins and you will always rank near the top of exciting expeditions in my life! I'm so glad you came to America and became part of our fun-but-crazy Stockberger/House clan... America and our family are so much the better for it! Thank you for the immense pleasure and privilege of entrusting the intimate details of your life to my writing. You are one very special man and I love you even more after this journey together!

To God be the glory!!!

The author, Terry Gray, and Vincent "Winnie" Nirich in 2009

"We are tied to the ocean.

And when we go back to the sea

– whether it is to sail or to watch it –

we are going back from whence we came."

President John F. Kennedy, September 14, 1962
Speaking at a dinner for the America's Cup crews

http://d-maps.com/carte.php?num_car=69052&lang=en

Croatia and the Adriatic Sea area

http://d-maps.com/carte.php?num_car=14902&lang=en

Prologue

July 25, 1956, approximately 11:10 pm.

The Atlantic Ocean off the New England coastline

Blood-curdling screams sliced through the dense foggy darkness, breaking the few seconds of eerie silence that had followed the violent jolt and ear-piercing squeals of metal on metal. Passengers who had just moments before been relaxing in their luxurious accommodations had been thrown out of their beds, their cabins crushed, trapping them inside where many of those unknowing vacationers would draw their last breaths.

The Italian luxury liner *SS Andrea Doria*, one of the most exquisite cruise ships of its day, had nearly completed a 9-day cross-Atlantic journey from her home port of Genoa to New York City. More like a floating museum, with unique ceramic décor and murals created by famous Italian artists, it was a cruise ship like no other and the first to feature three outdoor swimming pools, and over the years had become one of Italy's finest and most popular ocean liners filled to near capacity on almost every voyage. Engineered with comfort and stability in mind, the *Andrea Doria* was considered one of the safest ships to sail the seas and had made 100 successful Atlantic crossings during her 5-year life.

None of the 1,134 passengers and 572 crew members had any inkling that the 101st crossing would end so tragically. As the *Andrea Doria* raced through the dense fog toward the New York City harbor, the smaller Swedish ship *Stockholm* was heading westward under clear starry skies, apparently unaware of the thick fog bank she was about to enter. Many questions remain unanswered about exactly what caused the sea tragedy, most likely an unfortunate combination of thick foggy weather conditions, faulty radar, and questionable decisions by officers on both ships. But that fateful night just shortly after 11:10 pm., *Stockholm's* prow slammed into the starboard side of *Andrea Doria* dealing the mighty cruise ship a fatal blow, destroying many passengers' cabins, trapping their inhabitants inside and killing others on impact. Fifty-two known victims aboard the *Andrea Doria* perished as a result of the crash, and the other passengers and crew miraculously survived the ocean horror only through heroic rescue efforts, escaping via lifeboats before the *Andrea Doria* slipped under the waves to her dark watery grave at the bottom of the Atlantic eleven hours later.

It was a disaster of monumental proportions, and news of the horrific demise of the *Andrea Doria* flashed across the globe. Incredible survival stories became the stuff of news reports throughout America and the world. Several days passed before frantic families who had been separated during the melee were reunited in New York, and the ship's manifest was examined and an accounting had been made for all the passengers. The harbor pier was filled with many grief-stricken families when their immigrating relatives, looking to start a new life in America, were not among the survivors who made it to New York.

The sinking of *Andrea Doria* rocked the modern world.

♋ ♋ ♋ ♋ ♋ ♋ ♋ ♋ ♋ ♋

Across that same ocean in Yugoslavia, in the small Croatian seaside village of Stikovica, the shocking news spread like wildfire. Everyone was talking about the sea disaster, the unbelievable sinking of the well-known Italian luxury ocean liner. Stunned speechless, Ilija Njiric and his wife Franica snatched onto every tidbit of news they could about the *Andrea Doria* catastrophe, shocked and unwilling to comprehend what they knew to be true, their hearts sinking as surely and deeply as the *Andrea Doria* into the blackest depths.

They dared not breathe the fear that seized their souls. Their eldest child, their beloved teenaged son Visko, had been aboard the *Andrea Doria.*

CHAPTER 1

Born of the Sea

February 6, 1938

Stikovica, Dubrovnik, Yugoslavia

Briny waves gently lapped at the sides of the wooden fishing boat, licking its sun-bleached painted sides in a calm steady rhythm. The handmade boat was worn smooth with use, a raveling dingy rope mooring it against the constant assault of the incessant waves. Over its lifespan here on the edge of the Adriatic Sea, the boat had faithfully served the Njiric family both as a means of transportation to the nearby towns and villages as well as a source of livelihood, hauling nets full of fish over its sides to be sold in the town market.

Life in Stikovica revolved around the sea. Perched as it was on the side of the mountain, the Njiric family home sometimes seemed as one with the ocean, its tides and moods reflected in the ebb and flow of their daily lives. This strong, faithful fishing boat tied them to the bigger world beyond their four humble walls.

Most days, the boat was reliable transportation to the nearby town of Dubrovnik. Under Ilija's strong oar strokes, it was a mere three-mile sail across the bay to town, an easy trip for the young seasoned seaman. But on occasion when the waters were choppy, without other transportation, the family was forced to trade in that short boat ride for a 15-mile difficult hike along the rocky shoreline. Thankfully, those days were few and far between.

Franica pulled her woolen cloak as best she could around her swollen belly as she picked her way down the steep slope carefully, yet as quickly as she dared on the steadying arm of her Ilija. She broke her concentration briefly to glance down at the turquoise waters of the Adriatic Sea stretched out in front of her. So very beautiful, its teeming waters the bluest of blues, a familiar sight of which she never tired. Sandwiched between the sea breezes and the mountains, her village was protected from nature's extremes and even though the chill of winter was still in the air, February days were lovely. Today her sea was calm. For at least that small grace she could be grateful. But her smile was ever-so-brief as the next wave of contractions seized her, and she gripped Ilija's arm even tighter as she continued her downhill trek.

Their first child was making its way into this world, but despite all efforts of Franica's mother-in-law Amilija and the village midwife, the birth was not progressing as it should. After hours and hours of intense laboring and excruciating pain, this child was in no hurry to make its appearance, and finally the helpless and exasperated Ilija was called in to help them down to the dock. The fishing boat would take them to the hospital. Franica could only hope and pray that it wasn't too late.

After lifting his agonizing wife into the boat and into the caring arms of the midwife, Ilija untied the rope and pointed its prow toward Dubrovnik where they would get help at the hospital. Putting on a brave face, he tried not to show the panic that was threatening to suffocate him. His young wife and his firstborn child in grave danger, Ilija's brown sinewy arms pulled those oars like their very lives depended on it. Indeed, they did.

"Pozurite!   Beba dolazi!" the midwife urged as Franica writhed in pain at her side. *Hurry! The baby is coming!*

And it was there, in that faded fishing boat sluicing across waters of the Adriatic Sea, on Sunday, February 6, 1938, that Visko Ivo Njiric let out his first cry, blinking his bright blue eyes into the blinding sunshine.

Neither the newborn boy nor his family had any idea how prophetic Visko's birth was, in a rowboat, on the sea, that bright brisk February day.   In the many years ahead, the sea would be inexplicably intertwined with young Visko's life.

CHAPTER 2

Before the War

Spring 1941

Stikovica

Springtime's beauty ushered in a season of busyness for the Njiric household. The winters, though mild, kept the family inside more than other seasons of the year, and with the warmth of spring came longer daylight hours, the planting of the vegetable and flower gardens, extra work on the farm, and more frequent and longer commercial fishing trips for Ilija.

Little Visko, now a robust fellow of three years, had been joined a year later by his sister Cicilija who, unlike her older brother, was born without incident with the aid of the midwife in the seaside home. Franica had her hands full caring for two busy toddlers as well as keeping their home scrubbed clean, the gardens tended, and meals on the table. Visko's grandfather, the elder Visko Njiric (the toddler's namesake), and grandmother Amilija shared their home with the family.

The elder Visko, Grandpa Njiric, had led quite a colorful life himself before settling down in Stikovica in his later years. As a young man, he and his brother had been sold by their desperately poor parents as indentured servants, a practice all-too-commonplace among poor European families in the 19th century. Grandpa Njiric found himself working the first decades of his adult years for a wealthy cattle farmer in Chile, while his brother served elsewhere in South America. Communication in the mid-1800s was difficult, and many of the details of Grandpa Njiric's life in South America are probably best left to one's imagination. But suffice it to say that by the time the elder Visko earned his freedom after serving his contracted years, he returned to his Croatian homeland toting bags bulging with gold coins, quite a rich man.

Upon his return amid the swirling rumors about his new-found wealth, Visko Njiric married Amilija, and the two purchased a seaside lot, built a home, and set up housekeeping. When their son Ilija grew into a young man and wed Franica Durovic, a girl who hailed from high up in the mountains behind the village, the couple continued to live in Ilija's childhood home with Grandpa Visko and Grandma Amilija Njiric. It would be the same home where they reared their own family, which in a 14-year span eventually grew to include five children: the eldest son Visko, daughters Cicilija, Anita, Marica, and the youngest son Ivo.

While the Njiric family was rich compared to most of the other villagers, Grandpa Njiric put the majority of his gold in the bank, and they lived comfortably as any other villagers in serene Stikovica along the coastline of the Adriatic Sea. Although they didn't know any differently, daily life was difficult in that day and time with no plumbing, no electricity, and no transportation beyond their donkey and cart, mostly-bare feet, and their faithful fishing boat. Amilija and Franica grew lettuce, potatoes, onions, garlic, more lettuce, cabbages, tomatoes, more lettuce, beans, and other vegetables in their small but bountiful garden to accompany the suppers of fish they had nearly every day. The garden plot itself was not to be taken for granted, as the Njiric men had spent long tedious hours carrying bags of shoveled soil down the mountain to create a fertile spot amongst the rocky terrain. The farm consisted of many acres, most of which were untillable land up the steep mountainside behind their home. Besides a donkey, they also had a couple of pigs, a goat, a sheep, a cow for milk, and chickens for eggs to sell in town. Although the women carefully gathered eggs from their hens every day, the only time anyone in the family ever had the luxury of eating an egg was when they were sick. Then Grandma would mix up a concoction of a fresh egg, a little sugar or honey, and milk for the ailing person to drink. Eggs were money in the pocket, and a luxury meal in which they would not normally indulge.

photo from the Winnie Nirich collection

Three-year-old Visko was the eldest, with sister Cicilija doing her best to keep up with her active brother. Visko was the pride and joy of Grandpa Njiric, who often held Visko and Cicilija in his lap as he read Bible stories to them from a big worn book. Visko loved those cozy moments with his gentle grandfather, nestling into his iron arms and listening intently to his soothing soft voice. Already a couple of years past his hundredth birthday when his grandchildren were born, Grandpa Njiric was still a strong and vital man who had

Cicilija and Visko, circa 1942

lived a full life of work and adventure, with just a fringe of gray hair sticking out below his dirty captain's hat and his brown eyes still lively peering out beneath its worn brim. He carried a pocket watch in his woolen trousers, a token of his years in South America. One day many years later, young Visko would be entrusted with that very pocket watch as his only tangible reminder of his late grandfather.

A soft-spoken gentleman not easily riled, one would only realize that he was angry when Grandpa, without raising his voice, muttered curses in Spanish. No doubt he'd picked up the phrase from his many years amongst the Chilean workers. "Hombre carajo!" Surely his wife Amilija did not know the literal translation of his Spanish profanity; otherwise, Grandpa would not have gotten away with using such foul language in the home. But most times, Grandpa Njiric was a calm quiet gentleman, and little Visko basked in his attention and love, adoring this ancient man who was his grandfather.

"You can live all your life, you always learn something new." Grandpa's mantra was perhaps the secret to his longevity. Grandpa Njiric never stopped learning, even at the age of 105 when he met his bizarre end.

Little Visko had been only three years old when his mother took him into her arms and told him that his grandfather was dead. Grandpa Njiric's funeral marked the beginning of the traditional year of mourning for the Njiric family, with the women donning black clothing and men the traditional black arm patch, as their beloved patriarch was now gone. The elder Visko's death was as strange and unusual as his life had been. At 105 years old, he had been walking and working with the aid of his cane in the family's olive tree grove. Bottom branches of olive trees grew low and parallel to the ground, and Grandpa had climbed upon a lower branch so he could reach up and use his cane to pull one of the higher dead branches toward him, so he could prune it out. Teetering in this precarious pose, which he had surely struck scores of times before, Grandpa Visko Njiric lost his balance and fell out of the tree, suddenly killed when his poor old head smacked into a big rock. After a century-long life filled with crazy risk and mysterious adventure, Grandpa's quirky death was a tragic yet fitting end to his long, incredible life.

The Njiric family home was comfortable and utilitarian; its furnishings were sparse. A scraped-wood rectangular table sat in the corner of the dining room, flanked by wooden benches and a couple of straight-backed chairs. Sunlight reflecting off the sea streamed through the open windows, bouncing off the white-washed plaster walls and scrubbed marble floor, lighting the home and providing a most picturesque view. Unpretentious, the abode was cozy and inviting, and it was home. Franica spent much of her time preparing food in the two kitchens just off the dining room. In the farthest kitchen, adjacent to the barn, a raised open fire-pit was used for smoking and preparing meats and for baking the traditional cone-shaped bread under hot coals. In a second kitchen, closer to the living quarters, Grandma Njiric and Franica used a wood cookstove and a chairless wooden table for preparing meals which were served in the dining room. Without running water in the village, the homes were constructed with a built-in system of catching run-off water from the roof and funneling it inside the home into a lower-level cistern, where the family kept a live eel to eat the inevitable mosquito larvae that hatched in the water. Perhaps not the most sanitary of conditions, but it provided necessary water for the family's use.

Besides beds with cornhusk mattresses and pillow-tick covers for sleeping and a few religious pictures on the walls, the home boasted little else in the way of furniture. There was no need for anything else. One was either cooking, eating, working, or sleeping. No need nor time for soft chairs or relaxing. Grandma Njiric's chair was the closest concession to comfortable furniture, as her old bones had earned the soft pillow placed on its seat. Everything else in the home was plain and simple and served the family just fine.

But as safe and cozy a haven as the Njiric home was on the inside, outside in the village of Stikovica there was a restless unease. Powerful European countries around Yugoslavia had been rattling their sabers and rallying around the new German leader Adolf Hitler, and the war that was already raging in other parts of Europe now hung like a threatening dark cloud over the tiny village and indeed the whole Adriatic Sea area. War seemed inevitable, and although unwilling to engage and trying to maintain neutrality, it seemed impossible that Croatia and its neighboring states would ultimately be able to avoid involvement in the conflict.

The sight of foreign soldiers carrying guns in the streets became more commonplace, and the villagers tried their best to continue life as routinely as possible. The happy clatter and chatter in the streets was replaced by an ominous stifling restlessness, the light-hearted laughter turned to tense, forced smiles as folks went about their everyday business. War was coming to their home...one could feel it in the air.

One afternoon, in the arms of his mother Franica, little Visko watched wide-eyed as a group of Italian soldiers lingered on the cobblestone street. Even though the Italian military were friendly forces trying to help defend their Yugoslav neighbors, Grandma Njiric and Franica had admonished the children not to look at nor have anything to do with them. For some reason, on this particular day, the curious toddler had made eye contact with one soldier, and it brought a smile to the Italian's face. Having paused with his buddies for lunch, the Italian soldier held out a piece of bread spread with butter and jelly. Visko's eyes lit up with desire for the sweet treat, but he knew better than to speak or take things from strangers, especially strangers in military garb babbling in strange languages. He sought his mother's face to see how he should react, and with softened eyes and a faint glimmer of a smile, she nodded her head. That was all the permission he needed, and Visko grinningly accepted the delicacy from the soldier. It was his first close-up encounter with a foreign military man, and one he never forgot. Little did he or his mother realize how imminent and numerous their encounters with legions of foreign soldiers would be, most not nearly so friendly, in the days, months, and even years to come.

CHAPTER 3

Ousted

Late 1943

Stikovica

Calendars were a luxury. Little Visko had never even seen a calendar and, years later, he realized it would have been impossible anyway to remember exact times and dates when one's life has been turned upside down and inside out and every single moment takes immense effort just to survive. Especially when one is only five years old.

The war consumed Visko's family and indeed all of those living near Dubrovnik, forcing them into war's grim reality of life and death. The two were so closely intertwined that sometimes they almost seemed to merge. In April of 1941, when World War II had kept Europe under siege for 18 months already, Germany invaded Yugoslavia and over the past two years had crept closer and closer to the Adriatic Sea village where Visko's family lived. One morning late in the year of 1943, a group of German soldiers burst through the door into the Njiric home and ordered the family out. Immediately. Because of its strategic location and vantage point where the army could watch over the entire bay, the Nazis would use the Njiric home as a lookout.

Startled and terrified, Grandma and Franica sprang toward the frightened children who clung to their skirts. A baby girl, Anita, had joined the family the year before, a chub-cheeked darling that toddled around with her busy brother and sister. Grabbing the hands of young Visko and Cicilija and snatching Anita into her arms, Franica and Amilija held their heads down as they squeezed the wide-eyed little ones past the glaring Germans and out the door into the gravel street with little else but the clothes on their backs and a few items Grandma had hastily thrown into a bag. Franica's heart pounded with fear and uncertainty as she dared glance back at the home she adored, her lovely well-tended gardens and menagerie of livestock, wondering if she would ever lay her eyes on them again. Then teary-eyed but resolute, she straightened her shoulders, turned her face toward the mountain, and bravely began to lead her family up its steep narrow path. She would go to her childhood village of Pubreze high above the Adriatic Sea where they would stay with her parents, Givo and Ana Durovic, until the war was over, then they would return home. Franica had a plan.

Ilija was not present the day the Germans seized his family home. Ever since the war started, Ilija had become part of the underground Croatian resistance, the Cetniks, a loosely-organized and inadequately-armed group of men determined to defend their homeland. Fighting the enormous Nazi war machine head-on was impossible for these greatly out-numbered and under-armed young men, but they used ambushes, spies, and whatever unconventional means they could to disrupt the German war effort in Croatia. Brave, strong, and resourceful men they were, and many of them found employment working for the German soldiers, all the while using their positions to help The Underground and the Croatian people. Some worked for the Germans as mail couriers, taking official communications from village to village while secretly slipping personal notes to hiding families or Underground conspirators into their socks so as not to be discovered. Ilija found employment using his mariner skills, ferrying the Nazis from place to place across the water. The soldiers had no idea that Ilija was part of the underground resistance, nor did they have any clue that this uneducated Croatian sailor comprehended and memorized every word they were saying. Ilija pretended not to understand the Germans' conversations which often included war strategies, but in fact even though he never went to school, Ilija was fluent in six languages: Slavish/Croatian, Italian, German, French, Russian, and Polish. And so Ilija was able to provide pertinent information to his underground comrades about the enemies' whereabouts and schemes. Covering as a simple unschooled ferryman, Ilija was a spy.

Ilija was surely shocked and furious when he learned about the seizure of his home, but he was helpless against the conquering Nazis. The best way he could help his countrymen get their nation back was to serve as best he could in the underground resistance movement. He knew Franica and his mother Amilija, both capable and strong women, would do everything in their power to keep his family as safe as was possible in a country torn by war. While at first he wasn't sure where they had gone, he suspected correctly that Franica had fled to her family's home in Pubreze. He trusted that high up in the rugged mountains his family was probably out of harm's way, as the German army would not have reason nor desire to traverse the steep rocky trail.

Njiric home on the Adriatic Sea

photo by Vinnie Nirich

Grandpa and Grandma Durovic were alarmed to see their daughter Franica and her weary, frightened company on their stone doorstep. It had been an exhausting day's hike up the dangerously-narrow rugged path with three toddlers in tow. Grandma Durovic opened the door wide and as Franica fell into the soft familiar comfort of her mother's arms, the tears she had held in check began to fall uncontrollably. What their future held she was uncertain, where her beloved Ilija was she had no idea…all she knew is that she had made it, safe for now, to the haven of her childhood home. For that, she was grateful.

Franica, Grandma Njiric, Visko, and his two little sisters lived in the mountain home for several weeks. After a few days, the fear disappeared from Franica's face and her heart began to beat in a normal rhythm again. The nightmares slowly faded and Franica and her family settled into a daily routine in the humble mountain abode. Franica and Grandma Njiric helped prepare the meals and tend to the chores, while Visko and Cicilija played with their cousin Luko who lived there. Ilija stopped by the home when he was afforded the opportunity, and Franica relived for him that terrifying day that the Germans kicked them out. He'd been keeping an eye on his home, walking past whenever he got the chance, hoping that this military occupation would be short-lived and soon he'd be able to bring his family back to Stikovica, back to the comfortable home that Grandpa Visko Njiric had worked so hard to provide for his family. Surely the war wouldn't last too much longer…surely soon they'd all be able to put these horrible events in the past and go back to their quiet, peaceful life in their serene fishing village. Surely….

Those dreams were quickly dashed. Just a few short weeks after moving in with Franica's family, once more a contingent of German soldiers pounded through the door and ordered them all out. Caught in the déjà vu, Franica and Grandma Njiric once more hastily gathered a few items and the three small children, but this time they were also joined by Franica's parents as well as their grandson Luko.

And as the family made its way out of the home and into the street, they trickled into the stream of other villagers who had met the same fate... several households and families, all now scared, homeless, and trudging up the mountain path, wandering and wondering where they would lay their heads that night.

Mountains behind the Njiric home

photo by Zachary Nirich

No one recalls exactly whose idea it was, but someone suggested their best option was a large cave several miles from Pubreze. Half a day's hike in the best of circumstances, it took this ragged troupe twice as long, but finally they arrived at their destination. It would be a temporary respite from the elements for the hundred or so people, all either elderly, or women and children, as every able-bodied man was doing his part fighting with the Underground to rid their homeland of the invading Germans. They would stay in the cave for a short while, until the warring stopped, and they could return to their homes.

Franica and Grandma Njiric found an area along the edge of the big dark rock room to put down their meager belongings. So this would be home, for a few days anyway. The cave was cool and damp, but very spacious with tunnels leading off in different directions to other large underground rooms. A wonderful stream of fresh water ran through its middle, the same stream which would decades later become the principle water source for the seaside city of Dubrovnik. Fresh water was vital to their survival, and at least that necessity was covered. Someone had brought along a cow, so there was milk to drink. Most everyone was related somehow or another, so this cave became home to a huge extended family of mostly women and children, with a few old folks as well. The few items each family had managed to gather became common property, an assortment of pots and pans, blankets and clothing, and a few utensils. Community meals were cooked over a central fire, which also served as the only light inside the cave as well as its only source of heat. While it wasn't cold, the constant temperature in the 55-degree range along with the dampness that goes along with being inside the earth made for a constant chill in the air. However, they were out of the rain and sun, protected from the winter winds, and there was a sense of safety in numbers.

The youngest of the children didn't seem to mind at all. Cicilija and Anita had lots of new playmates, and they spent their days playing together in the dirt and gravel just outside the cave. But the "older" boys, those too young to fight, didn't have time for playing. Theirs was the most crucial role of all.

CHAPTER 4

Scavengers

1944

Croatian mountain cave

Six-year-old Visko sat at the cave entrance with his cousins in the twilight, listening to the cracking of gunfire and faint shouting in the distance. Excitedly the boys compared notes, their ears fine-tuned by now to determine the direction from which the echoing shots had come. They'd been at this for several months now and were quite efficient at their task. As soon as the shooting ended and morning broke, they would head down the mountain in that very direction.

Where there had been shooting, there would be dead German soldiers. And where there were dead soldiers, there would be food.

Now six, Visko was the youngest of this band of four boys, with his nine-year-old cousin Branko being the leader and the oldest. Joining them were Stijepon and sometimes Luko, Visko's cousins from nearby villages. Occasionally they'd allow another lad or two to come along, but for most expeditions it was just those three or four. Too many feet make too much noise, and the last thing they ever wanted to do was to attract attention. The boys prided themselves on their stealthy tactics, and that is most probably what kept them alive.

Upon the homeless villagers' arrival at the cave, it didn't take long for the meager food supplies that they had brought along to dwindle away. Feeding one hundred hungry mouths takes a lot of food. Early on, it was obvious that someone would have to find food for them all, as it would be impossible for their menfolk to keep them supplied. Even if the men had had plenty of food available (which they didn't), they were trying to stay alive themselves as they fought with the Underground. Those most able to slip by German soldiers unheeded were the children.

So small bands of children were sent out to scavenge for food, Visko's group being one of those bands. Leaving with only the clothes they were wearing for several days at a time, Franica could hardly bear to watch her son and his friends go, yet there was really no other choice. Someone had to provide food or they would all starve; it was as simple as that. The young boys were the cave community's best chance for survival. Most days, Franica had no idea where her little Visko was, and every time she sent him off her heart broke at the thought that perhaps she would never see him again, a very real possibility. Finding food in a war zone was a perilous proposition.

For Visko and his group, every time out was a new adventure. Oftentimes they would go back to Pubreze, the village to which the Njirics had fled when the Germans first seized their home. Even with their energetic young legs, that trek was a hard half-day's hike. While they were in the mountain scrub, they didn't worry too much about being discovered. But as they got closer and closer to the village, the boys began to pick their steps ever-so-carefully. One of the boys went ahead of the rest, serving as a scout and calling out an animal-sound alarm if there was danger ahead. They must not be heard, for if they were heard, their mission would be over before it even began. And they could never return to the cave empty-handed. Never.

Perched tightly against the steep mountain slope, the half dozen homes that made up Pubreze were backed up right into the mountainside, with the windows on the back of the homes being just a couple of feet off the ground. Access was easy for the young marauders, as the glassless windows were open or, at most, covered with a thin screen of chicken wire that was quickly torn away. The hard part was stealing the food without being seen. After checking to be sure the coast was clear, Visko, being the smallest, would scramble through the thick window opening, dropping down quietly onto the floor below and searching the kitchen while the others let down a rope through the window. Visko would tie whatever he could find, perhaps a sack of flour or rice, onto the end of the rope and the older boys would pull the rope up, untie the goods, and send it back down for another load. Small items were stuffed in Visko's pockets or tossed into a bag he might find. Then Visko clung to the rope as his accomplices pulled him up and back out the window. The goal was to steal what you could but not so much that it would be noticed. After stashing their loot in a safe place to retrieve later, they would move on to the next home. All the while, the scout and other boys would constantly be on the lookout for approaching German soldiers who would put a quick end to their stealing spree and send them all hastily retreating back into the dense mountain undergrowth until the danger was gone.

For such young tender minds, the boys had put together an ingenious scheme that worked flawlessly almost every time. After they'd made the rounds and hauled up as much food as they knew they would be able to carry, the four of them packed up their goods on their backs and shoulders and started the long walk back to the cave, stopping along the path to spend the night under the stars when it became too dark to see and their little bodies too weary to take another step. When they arrived back at their cave the next day, they received a hero's welcome as everyone was eager to see what they'd brought back with them. Most often there was little to feed the exhausted boys even after all their work, and they'd lie down hungry, falling asleep nearly before their heads hit the warm rock that served as their beds. Then the next day, they'd be up early and headed out again.

One day as Visko was dropping in through a window, he startled a soldier who was stationed as a guard inside the home. Visko froze in terror as he and the Nazi soldier locked eyes for a brief moment; then the soldier turned his back on Visko and looked the other way. It was the fastest food heist ever, as Visko very quickly and deftly tied a smoked side of pork onto the rope and climbed on with it as his friends pulled them both through the safety of the window before they high-tailed it out of there. There was no doubt that the German saw him and knew what he was up to, but even amidst the cut-throat world of war, human compassion sometimes shows up in the most unexpected ways.

But for every compassionate German soldier, there were ten who were not. One day, as Visko was beginning to tie his food find onto the rope, he turned around to see a smirking soldier watching him. The rope quickly disappeared through the window, but Visko had no time to hop aboard. The German soldier grabbed the food away from Visko, snarling, "Aussteigen!" as he pointed toward the open door. *"Get out!"* With a swift kick to Visko's backside, the soldier's thick leather army boots sent the boy sprawling across the room. Hitting the wall hard, there was no time to rub his sore bottom as Visko struggled to his bare feet and scurried out the door and around the house as fast as his trembling legs could carry him. He didn't stop running up the rocky mountainside until he could run no more, finally collapsing onto the ground to get his breath. It was a close call, but he was safe. His friends had vamoosed with the food at the first sight of the German, but Visko eventually met back up with them. Frightened but undaunted, they were soon at it again. There was no giving up...their family depended on the boys.

Visko's uncle had been a beekeeper and had several beehives just outside Pubreze village. Occasionally, Visko and company would raid the hives and bring back that sweet delicacy to the cave-dwellers, acquiring a few inevitable beestings in the process. But one taste of that sticky golden treat on a crumb of Franica's bread made it all worthwhile.

Using a wooden club as their only weapon, the boys killed any small wildlife that came their way and could be used as food. Rabbits, raccoons, and minks were often victims of a blow to their heads, and the boys were thrilled to add some meat to their plunder. Once, Visko and his friends came upon two young wild pigs which they were able to kill, but they didn't stick around because where there are baby pigs a big protective mother pig is sure to be close by, and the young boys were certainly not prepared to meet a mad wild hog head-on. If they happened upon a bird's nest, they'd stick the unhatched eggs in their pockets which were later given as a special nutritional treat to the pregnant women in the cave. Sparrows and small birds didn't have much meat on them, but they were better than nothing, and the boys killed them whenever they had the chance. Meat was meat, and the villagers were hungry enough to eat anything the resourceful boys brought back.

Home raids occupied most the boys' days, unless they heard gunshots in the distance. Those days were special and Visko knew that a fruitful adventure was ahead. Underground Croatian fighters would often ambush Nazi soldiers and a fierce battle would ensue, inevitably leaving some of those Germans dead on the ground. The well-equipped German army kept its soldiers fed, and the boys quickly discovered that each one of those soldiers bore a canvas tube-shaped bag connected to a leather strap slung across their bodies. And inside that canvas bag were military rations...cans of beans, corned beef, bread, and cigarettes...a pure treasure trove for starving villagers. A good long skirmish meant there would be several dead soldiers, and the boys clambered over the cold stiff uniformed bodies to cut away the leather straps, tying the straps together and hanging the food-filled bags over their own shoulders to carry back to the cave. The boys didn't bother taking the soldiers' watches, money, or even their weapons. Food was all they were after; coins or guns do not fill empty bellies.

Only one time did Branko take one of the soldier's guns, thinking he would shoot an animal. He built a stand for the gun and baited a rabbit with a couple of carrots. The rabbit came and Branko shot it as the younger boys looked on, but the powerful weapon blew the bunny into smithereens. So much for that idea.

Kicking along a deserted road one afternoon, a German soldier came out of nowhere, startling Visko. "Where are you going?" he demanded, grabbing the boy's shirt.

Shaking with fear, Visko managed a quick cover-up. "I'm going to my aunt's house in the next village."

"What is your aunt's name?" The big German's eyes bored a hole through Visko.

Visko shuffled his feet in the dirt, and without looking up told the soldier his aunt's name, that she was old and sick in the village, and that he was going to see her. It wasn't a complete lie…his aunt was indeed in the next village, unable to travel with the rest of her family. But Visko certainly wasn't planning to stop in for a visit when he had work to do. The German looked him over, decided the dirty runt of a boy wasn't worth his time and trouble, and walked away.

Every once in a while, the Underground fighters would bring some food to their families in the cave, to supplement the boys' finds. Not only were the villagers starving for the cheese and food stuffs their menfolk would bring them, they were also starving for news from their loved ones and the war. Was there any word from so-and-so? Have you seen so-and-so? How much longer would it be before they could return to their homes? Some may have answers to the first questions, but no one knew the answer to the last one. Occasionally, a young man on horseback would ride up bringing messages or news. Once, the horseback messenger told Franica that Ilija wanted her to meet him at a certain place and a certain time, so Franica left her children in their grandmothers' care and was gone down the mountain for a couple of days. Any contact with the world outside those cavernous rock walls was welcome and raised the spirits of the villagers, giving them hope that someday soon the war would be over, and life would return to normal.

But until that happened, the boys faithfully continued venturing out on their food-finding missions. Few and far between were any type of confrontations with the German soldiers. That's how sneaky and smart those boys were, and they were able to scrounge up enough food to keep most of those living in the cave alive to finally see the end of the war.

CHAPTER 5

A Taste of America

September 1945

Zaton Bay, Adriatic Sea

Seasons came and went, and the cave community coped as best they could. Talk always revolved around the war, wondering aloud how fathers and husbands and sons were faring in this fighting that continued to rage below them and indeed all across Europe and the world. Visko had heard his grandfathers and father speak of The Great World War that had happened at the turn of the century. This war, which came to be known as World War II, had already exploded into an even bigger and more deadly one.

As new babies were born in the cave, old folks died. The old men painstakingly chipped out shallow temporary graves from the rocky ground just outside the cave, piling rocks on top to bury the bodies. After the war, the remains would be removed and carried down the mountain to be laid to rest alongside their ancestors.

Visko had never seen snow. Living in the mild climate of the Adriatic Sea, snow only happened once in a century or so and many people lived their entire lives along the seashore without ever seeing a snowflake. But up in the mountains where the cave was, snow was a normal wintertime occurrence. It was while living in the cave that

Visko first saw the magical white stuff falling from the sky. At first he was mesmerized by its quiet mysterious beauty, but it didn't take long for him to realize that foraging for food was even harder when one was barefoot in the snow. Winter was a long and hungry season.

Hunger was a constant companion to young Visko. Returning to the cave after several days of searching for food, the boys turned their stash over to their mothers and grandmothers to divvy out amongst the villagers. The babies and sick were cared for first, and often when mealtime came there was very little left over for the healthy boys. Visko was always hungry.

"It is good to go to sleep hungry," Franica told her little boy. "Food in your belly would cause nightmares." How it must have broken her heart to send Visko to his rock bed with that fib, but he accepted it as truth and exhausted sleep won out over his grumbling empty stomach.

Exactly how long they lived in the cave, Visko was uncertain...somewhere between a year and eighteen months, as all four seasons went through their rotation at least once. But one blessed day in the fall of 1945, an older Croatian gentleman galloped his horse to the cave entrance and announced the words they had all waited for months and months to hear: "The war is over. You can return to your homes."

Could it really be true?! Undoubtedly some must have wondered if this news was just a cruel hoax, but the horseback messenger insisted that he had been sent by The Underground to bring their families back home, so the villagers in excited anticipation packed up what little they had and began their descent down the mountain and back to their home villages.

For Visko and his family, that meant a 12-mile trek down a steep, rocky mountain path. Franica and Grandma Njiric led the three children, seven-year-old Visko, six-year-old Cicilija, and little three-year-old Anita, back down the same route they had fearfully and tearfully traveled nearly two years before. This time the fear was still present but it was a different kind of fear, a fear of the unknown and what they would find when they arrived in Stikovica. And this time the tears were much different, they were tears of joy. The Njiric family was returning home!

By this time, Visko was as sure-footed as a mountain goat, but the rest of his family was not able to scramble from rock to rock as quickly and confidently as he. Often, he became impatient with their slow pace and rambled ahead, but Franica would call his name and reign him back to stay with the rest of the clan. As they followed the twisted path, they carefully watched their steps lest someone slip on some loose rocks and tumble down the mountainside. Occasionally, after rounding a bend in the path, they could catch sight of the sparkling turquoise waters of their beloved Adriatic Sea and tiny specks that must be boats and people milling around. But what was that gray object in the water, still small itself but dwarfing the other objects nearby?

Hours passed, and at each bend, the sea became a little closer and the gray object a little bigger. A ship! It must be a ship, perhaps a remnant from the war. Little Visko could hardly contain his curiosity! Yes, it was a ship; he could see now. A battleship, hopefully not German. The courier had assured them that the war was over, so surely this must be a friendly ship, one belonging to Yugoslavia's allies.

As the path finally widened and leveled out and Stikovica came into sight, Visko bolted down the rest of the way heading straight for the seashore. With each stride the boat loomed larger and larger to the little boy, and by the time he reached the docks that ship seemed to completely take up the whole bay. Enormous gray metal sides bristling with guns sticking out and its prow pointing straight toward the Njiric home, the war ship miniaturized the faded-paint rowboat where Visko had spent much of his life. Visko had never seen anything like it, more magnificent and powerful than he could ever have imagined. He was staring in awe at the monstrosity sitting in his bay when his cousin Mladen, who had been living with his aunt in Dubrovnik during the war, ran up to Visko.

Pointing excitedly at the ship, Mladen greeted Visko. "Get on that ship! Go! They will give you anything you want to eat!"

Emaciated Visko, who hadn't had a full belly in 18 months, didn't need any encouragement. A rowboat was ferrying groups of people to the ship, and Visko wormed his way into line to get on one of those rowboats. Some villagers were afraid as they'd never seen a battleship before, but Visko couldn't get there quickly enough. The man in charge allowed one person from each family to go to the ship, and Visko jumped aboard the rowboat as the Njiric representative. That ship looked even more massive from the seat of the rowboat, and Visko marveled wide-eyed as the oarsman brought his straggly load of war-torn villagers across the water to the ship.

Visko smelled the bread long before he ever saw it. A ladder dropped into the rowboat from the side of the ship, and the most wonderful smell in the world filled the air. Visko followed that delicious aroma up the ladder, across the plank, into the ship, through the metal hallways, and to the kitchen. As he popped his head inside the ship's galley, loaves of freshly-baked white bread were lined up on the shelf. Visko had never even seen white bread before, as Franica always baked cornbread for her family. Uniformed sailors babbled strange words as they handed sandwiches to the hungry peasants, but the smell of that bread spoke Visko's language, and without waiting his turn for a sandwich he snatched an unsliced loaf of that warm white bread and began eating it as fast as he could bite and swallow. Never had bread tasted as scrumptious as on that day! Visko neither noticed nor cared, but the sailors were amused and entertained watching this seven-year-old boy eat so heartily, and one of them handed Visko a glass bottle of dark liquid to wash the bread down.

A 7-ounce bottle of Coca-Cola. Visko had no idea what it was, but he took a sip and the strange, bubbly sweetness danced on his tongue and tickled his throat all the way down. It was the most delicious drink he'd ever had, and between bites of bread he gulped down the bottle of Coke. For the first time in nearly two years, his belly was full! But it didn't take long for the hunger pains to be replaced by stomach cramps, as his little starved body rebelled at the sudden yeasty bread/carbonated, sugary drink combination. Visko was sick all over and wondered if he'd been poisoned; in his zeal for food he'd gone overboard, and it didn't take long for him to regret the painful lesson. Not a good idea to eat a whole loaf of bread and wash it down with Coca-Cola, especially on a hunger-shrunken empty stomach.

His belly full but aching, Visko was handed a bag filled with food as he left the ship. Down the ladder he climbed, carrying back to his waiting family powdered eggs, packages of chicken soup, cans of corned beef, a few loaves of bread, and other sundry food items, the makings of feasts for the Njiric supper table for many days to come.

"I don't know where that ship comes from, but I'm going there," Visko exclaimed to his cousin Mladen as he got out of the rowboat onto the Stikovica piers. "If their ships can feed everybody in the world, they must be a great rich country."

Visko found out after he walked into the village that the ship was American, a United States destroyer. Just a young lad at the time, Visko had barely heard of that place on the other side of the world called America, but right then and there at the tender age of seven years old, Visko decided that's where he was going.

CHAPTER 6

New Beginnings

1946

Stikovica

The war was over, but the scars left behind were deep and would take years to heal. Franica and Grandma Njiric were devastated as they walked into their once clean and organized home. While Visko was aboard the American ship, the women took inventory of the life they had left behind nearly two years before. The Germans were gone, but the departing soldiers had ransacked homes, killed all the livestock, and destroyed everything they could before leaving. Anything of any value was gone, presumably taken by the soldiers as they left.

The once-lovely Njiric home was in shambles. Furniture was bashed with splintered pieces of wood thrown about in every room. In Grandma's bedroom, her bed was shattered into pieces, pictures from her wall thrown down; her dresser that she kept locked had been torn apart, and its contents scattered across the marble floor.

Outside, it was eerily quiet. No roosters crowing, cows mooing, or sheep bleating...there were no animals anywhere, not even a roaming cat or dog. What The Underground hadn't used for food, the Germans had killed or the Italians, who had come into

Yugoslavia to help restore order following the utter destruction of the war, had butchered. The village of Stikovica was turned upside down, and the villagers slowly began putting their lives back together as best they could

Yugoslavia, officially the Federal People's Republic of Yugoslavia, was now solidly a Communist country. Directly after the war ended, the monarchy was abolished and a new Communist government was established with Josip Broz Tito firmly in power as the new Yugoslavian President. Six separate republics had been forced to combine to form the new Communist nation, with Bosnia, Macedonia, Montenegro, Slovenia, and Serbia joining Croatia. It would remain this way until the early 1990s when Yugoslavia broke apart along the republics' boundaries, becoming separate nations again when the Yugoslav Wars broke out.

President Tito, while a Communist leader, was generally well-liked by the Croatians. Even though there was always subtle pressure to join the Communist party, people were not coerced to join and the Njiric family never did. The rules were a little stricter and job opportunities a bit more limited if one wasn't Communist, but President Tito brought stability to the area and everyday life in Stikovica was only mildly affected by the new political regime. Fishing and farming people didn't need anything from the government and offered little to the national economy, so the villagers continued on with the same way of life as they had for centuries before. And the government, beyond collecting taxes, pretty much left them alone.

Now that the war was over, the underground resistance fighters disbanded and went back to their village lives. Ilija, with the help of Visko and Cicilija, worked hard to begin cleaning up the farm and getting the olive trees and grapevines, which had not been tended during the war years, pruned and trimmed for the next growing season's harvest. Ilija also began his commercial fishing trips again, going out two or three times a week bringing in fish to sell at the market. Gradually, he was able to buy another cow, a few chickens, and some other livestock for the farm. Slowly, slowly over time, the Njiric life became much as it was before the war, with one huge exception.

Before the war, the Njirics had been rich with quite a lot of money in the bank; during the war, the former monarchy had taken all the money out of the banks and given it to the ousted royal family who were now living in Austria. All that gold, Grandpa Njiric's nest egg that he'd brought home from South America decades ago, was gone, and there was nothing the enraged Ilija could do about it. Just like that, the family had gone from wealth to poverty. For the rest of his life, Ilija would never trust banks again and secretly squirreled his extra money away in hiding places known only to him and years later to his sons.

Despite their huge financial nosedive, the resilient family began to put the pieces of their war-torn life back together. There was really no other choice. Although Ilija desperately had hoped for another son, Franica gave birth to their fourth child and third daughter Marica in 1946. Counting his mother Grandma Amilija Njiric, there were now seven mouths for Ilija to feed and certainly no time to feel sorry for himself. Like everyone around him, Ilija worked long hard days, and with the help of Franica and the children there was always food on the table and a place to lay their heads at night. As they'd proved over and over again, the Njirics were survivors.

After the war, Ilija discovered another profitable enterprise to bring in money for his family. He'd heard some of the village men whispering about black market runs, and he decided to join them. Although risking severe punishment from the government if caught, there had never been a time in his life when risk had deterred Ilija. Just off the shore between Croatia and Italy was a small island with a lighthouse, which separated Yugoslavian waters from international waters. A group of men, on the pretense of a fishing trip, would row over to the small island and throw out their nets during the daytime. But then at night, they would use six-oarsmen racing sculls for a quick trip to Italy, where they would spend a day purchasing items that were impossible to find in Yugoslavia. The men brought back cigarettes, playing cards, pepper, and the hottest item of all (bringing upwards of fifty to seventy-five dollars per pair back home) nylon stockings, especially the black stockings featuring little embroidered designs, over which the city women went crazy. After rowing back to the island in the cover of night, they'd pick up their nets in the morning and return home…maybe with a few fish to peddle, but much more importantly many contraband treasures to sell for big bucks in the Dubrovnik marketplace.

Visko, now eight years old, began formal schooling for the first time in his life. A smart little boy and certainly wise and life-experienced way beyond his years, Visko found book-learning to be much more challenging than he expected. Although mathematics came easily to Visko's analytical, problem-solving young mind and he used his natural math skills often to make change and figure weights when Franica would take him to the market to sell items while she shopped, apparently the other skills he had honed that kept his family alive during the war were not very useful in the classroom. Reading and writing were difficult. Visko found it hard to sit still, and his mischievous mind and antics kept him much more often in the teacher's bad graces than her good.

The school was in Zaton Mali, across the bay, a walk of about three miles or so around the shoreline for Visko and Cicilija. The main road ran right in front of their house, so the two young Njiric children would join in the daily stream of children from other villages and down off the mountain who were walking to school. The school day began at 7:00 and ended at 11:00 every morning except for Sundays, nine months out of the year with the summer months off. By 7 am. Visko had already been up for three hours. Up every morning at 4:00 before the sun even thought about peeking over the hilltops, Visko crawled out of bed into his clothes as it was his daily chore to lead the cow and goat, with the sheep and occasional donkey following along, a couple of miles up the mountainside of their farm to a stone wall enclosure where they would spend the day grazing until Visko came again in the evening to lead them back down to the barn for the night. When he came back down the mountain path each morning, Visko joined Cicilija at the table for a breakfast of fruit or cheese or a piece of toast before heading off to school for the morning, carrying his small dinged-metal pail that Franica packed with a snack for the daily 9:30 break, perhaps some cheese, an onion, or a piece of bread, maybe a chunk of lard or smoked pork, whatever she had on hand from the previous evening's supper.

Inside the school, Visko sat with other children in one big room with one teacher for grades one through six. The large room was partitioned off into three smaller ones, separating the first- and second-graders from the third- and fourth-graders as well as the fifth- and sixth-graders. Their teacher, a very serious strict lady, could see all her students at once from her desk at one end of the room, but because of the partial walls they couldn't see each other. Eight other first-graders were in Visko's class, children with whom he had grown up and known his entire life.

Visko and his teacher butted heads early on and often during the next six years. "Kapo Jundo," she called him in her brusk hostile voice, *"Leader of the Trouble."* From Day One, she kept a very close eye on Visko and quite often smacked him across his left palm with her painful pomegranate switch for any infraction. To say the two didn't like each other was an understatement, and Visko learned early how to get under her skin and couldn't resist the temptation to do so whenever the opportunity presented itself.

One incident in particular Visko would never forget. The schoolteacher wore to school one day a brand new pair of black nylon stockings with a little appliqued flower on the side, an expensive luxury bought most probably from the same black market in which Ilija and his friends dealt. At that time, if a lady was lucky enough to obtain a pair of stockings, women would come from everywhere to "ooh-and-aah" over such a magnificent silky treasure that most peasants could never dream of owning. In a very unfortunate set of circumstances that particular day, when his teacher brought down her pomegranate switch toward Visko's palm to punish him for yet another misbehavior, he quickly jerked his hand away at the last second causing the branch to hit the teacher's own leg, snagging a hole in those black nylons. She looked down in horror, and Visko's heart sunk as they both watched a huge white stripe trickle up her black-stockinged leg as the run quickly raced up the length of the hose until it disappeared beneath her black skirt. Visko slowly lifted his eyes in dread to meet the glaring horrified eyes of his teacher, knowing right then and there that his very life was in danger. All because of a pair of black embroidered nylon stockings.

The other children watched the scene in silent disbelief. "School is over. Go home." Teacher barked angrily at her students, who quietly gathered up their belongings and slunk out the door, heading home when the school morning was only half over. Visko grabbed his things as well and tried to disappear into the throng of schoolchildren as they poured out into the street. Usually babbling and happy, the students stepped quickly and quietly lest anyone else incur more of their teacher's wrath. Not far behind them marched Teacher, and Visko knew without a doubt where she was going, so he took the long route home in hopes of avoiding the inevitable.

When he finally had the nerve to go home, his father Ilija wasn't there, but Franica met him at the door. The look on her face told him all he needed to know. "Run somewhere, you better do something because your dad is going to kill you when he gets home." It wouldn't be the first beating Visko had gotten at the hands and belt of his father, but it was one of the most memorable. If Ilija didn't have a belt handy, he'd take the metal-ringed leather strop used for sharpening his razor to Visko's backside, once beating him so badly that the boy couldn't sit down for three days.

Another time the class had been working on a project building a model sailboat with tall masts and sails, a boat like the ancient mariners would have captained. Visko clumsily bumped into it, accidentally knocking it off the table and breaking it, earning himself another smacking from the schoolteacher. Visko got in trouble so many times, he came to expect a daily whack or two whether he needed it or not.

Kneeling in rock salt was another of Teacher's punishments. In the corner of the schoolroom was a pile of rock salt intentionally spilt across the wooden floor. Visko would have to roll up his long pants so his knees were bare and kneel in that pile, the sharp edges of the rock salt cutting into his skin, and the salt seeping into the cuts left behind. Despite wincing in pain, he could not make a sound and was forced to stay on his knees until the teacher gave him permission to get up. One would think that after a while Visko would learn his lesson, but even when he really tried, it seemed the ornery little rascal was always in some sort of trouble.

Visko's reputation as a trouble-maker didn't end at the schoolhouse doors. Grandma Njiric, upon hearing any news of mischief from the village was immediately convinced that her Visko was surely involved if not the instigator of the trouble, even if he was totally innocent of wrong-doing. Grandma would sit in her rocking chair in the corner of the dining room with her own long pomegranate-branch switch, just waiting for Visko to cross to go from the kitchen upstairs to the bedrooms. Waiting and watching as she silently rocked, as hard as Visko tried to time his escape with her rocking rhythm in an attempt to avoid the stinging switch, Grandma's timing was always accurate and her switch flicked him painfully across his body or face as he ran toward the stairs. A mean woman she was, hardened by life, and it seemed Grandma Njiric chose to vent her miseries on poor Visko.

Visko may not have tended to his book lessons as well as he should have, but in his eight short years on earth, he'd already learned a whole boatload of life lessons. And one of them was resilience, which would come in a whole lot handier than all that reading and writing and arithmetic.

photo from the Winnie Nirich collection

Cicilija, Anita, and Visko
Circa 1946

CHAPTER 7

Boy of Land and Sea

1948

Stikovica

"Race you to the blue boat!" Visko yelled to his cousin Branko, plunging into the turquoise Adriatic waters before the words had barely left his mouth. Branko plunged in beside him, the two boys slicing through the clear waters as smoothly and efficiently as any sea creature. Reaching the sun-bleached boat anchored in the bay, Visko barely beat his older cousin, and the two of them splashed water friskily at each other before whipping around and lazily kicking back to shore.

The sea was where Visko was the happiest; it seemed he was one with the blue waters. Just a few short months after his birth in the middle of the Adriatic Sea ten years prior, long before he took his first steps on land, Ilija had gently tossed his infant son into the water from his rowboat. Baby Visko sputtered for air, flailing his tiny arms and legs as the briny sea water kept him buoyant, and in a few short minutes Visko had learned to swim. And he hadn't stopped swimming since.

Such was the case with all the village children born at the edge of the sea. Swimming was a necessity of life, and with the saltwater keeping them afloat the babes learned quickly and effortlessly to swim. Being in the water came so naturally to Visko and his friends, they were amused when their mountain cousins learned to swim using a belt of dried gourds to keep their heads above water. For the Njiric family, the sea was their world, and Visko's heart would be forever bound to those crystal blue waters.

Ilija was a fisherman, a farmer, an entrepreneur, and a schmoozer. "Puho," they called him. *"Bag of air."* It was a fitting nickname for the rugged man in his sea captain's hat, a moniker which made him proud. There was little that happened in Stikovica, Zaton Mali, or even Dubrovnik of which Puho was unaware. It seemed to Visko that Ilija knew everyone and everyone knew Ilija, and indeed everyone did. His loud boisterous ways brought pride to Visko, but he was more than a little afraid of his gruff father too and tried his best not to cross him.

Two or three times a week, and always on Thursdays, Ilija and Visko would climb into their fishing boat late in the evening and row out to drop their nets, then head back home for a few hours of sleep. Seems he'd barely close his eyes before Ilija would be rousing Visko out of his warm bed and into the chilly dark predawn air, and they'd clamber down the rocky shoreline to the boat. Lit only by the stars overhead and a lantern in the boat, Ilija and Visko would push off into the black licking waters toward their nets marked by bobbing floats. Friday was a big market day for fish, as all the Catholic families in the villages served fish on Fridays, so Ilija was always hopeful for a big catch to fill the family coffers for another week.

Visko's job was to hold the boat still in the water while his dad pulled in the nets, a task not as simple as it might seem. As Ilija heaved on the bulging nets, the boat inevitably rocked back and forth in the waves, and it was all Visko could do to pull the oars first one way then another to try and keep it steady for his father. Ilija demanded perfection and more often than not, Visko could not hold the boat still enough to suit him and became the object of his father's aggravation. But eventually, Ilija would finally haul the last section of net into the boat, both boy and man sinking back against the weathered boards breathing heavily with exhaustion from fighting the waves and the weight of the catch. And Visko gladly handed the oars back to Ilija, watching the dying fish flop in the bottom of the boat as the shore drew closer and closer while the sun's early morning rays just began peeking into the darkness over the mountains.

Friday was market day, and most often not a school day for Visko. When he was needed at home to work, time to go to school was a luxury the family could not afford. After breakfast, Visko helped his father sort through the fish, keeping the biggest and best for market, a few for the family, and the fish that weren't sellable or edible they kept for bait. Tuna, mackerel, lobsters, and crabs would bring good money in Dubrovnik. Seafood was a staple for the Croatian folks, and fishermen like Ilija counted on that.

The Adriatic Sea teemed with all kinds of sea life. Dolphins were everywhere, and despite their smiling, friendly faces they were not welcomed by the fishermen. Most often torn and ripped nets could be blamed on dolphins, and torn nets meant down time for the fishermen to make repairs. Ilija didn't have much patience for that, but it was a necessary evil in the life of a fisherman, and Visko learned early to help his father fix the torn nets.

Farther out, near the island where the black marketers rendezvoused, Visko would occasionally see a whale spouting. He loved to watch the whales, fascinated by their graceful massiveness mysteriously hidden just beneath the water's surface. With only the steady rhythm of the waves breaking the silence, Visko could usually hear a whale or smell its fishy blow before he even saw it. Occasionally, the villagers would discover the treasure of a dead whale floating in the sea and haul it into the shore, where they would cut it up and use the fat to make soap and whale oil for lanterns.

Whales were magnificent creatures, and Visko never tired of the thrill of seeing one, dead or alive.

Indeed the sea was full of magnificent creatures, most of which became food on the Njiric table. Octopuses were plentiful and easily caught. Trolling along in the boat, Visko would slowly skim above the clear shallow waters, watching for an octopus moving along the ocean floor. Steadying the boat right over the creature, Visko gigged the octopus with a homemade five-pronged spear and pulled the writhing animal into the boat. If he had a knife, Visko stabbed the unfortunate creature between the eyes, but more times than not he had no knife, so he'd bite the octopus in the same spot to kill him, all the while dodging those eight suckered tentacles that were trying to wrap themselves around the boy. A small octopus was easily killed, but the bigger ones sometimes presented quite a wrestling match.

One day as he was walking home from school, a humongous octopus in the bay caught Visko's eye. He wasn't going to let this one get away! Quickly he threw down his books, stripped off his shirt, and dove into the water after it. A few minutes later he surfaced and, even though he was a strong swimmer, Visko struggled for the shore, as the octopus wrapped its long tentacles over his head and around his arms, trying to snake their way around his neck and into his mouth. Visko repeatedly bit it between the eyes as the octopus used its final dying efforts attempting to strangle Visko, squeezing suction marks all over the boy's body leaving bruises that would last for several days. Visko kept fighting and biting, and eventually the tentacles relaxed their grip on the frightened boy, and he had quite an octopus to take home to Franica that afternoon, the makings of a few delicious meals for the family.

Menu options for a large octopus were many for a creative cook like Franica. She put a huge pot of water on the fire and put the dead creature into the boiling water head first. Franica could tell when the octopus was cooked to perfection when the little suction cups on the tentacles began to come off. Sliced into bite-size pieces, the octopus tentacles added chewy nutrition to a big bowl of fresh lettuce and vegetables or were delicious in a soup or even on their own. Visko's fight with the strong-armed octopus was worth it when he tasted it on their dinner table that evening.

Sardines were another staple of the villagers' diet. For as long as Visko could remember, a 55-gallon wooden barrel filled with salted sardines sat in the corner of the kitchen, alongside a matching barrel filled with cabbages used, among other things, to make sauerkraut. Oftentimes Visko would find a sardine or two with cheese in his lunch pail or alongside vegetables for lunch or supper. Pulling off the heads would gut the small fish simultaneously and a quick rubbing with a leaf or finger took off the soft scales, but usually Visko would just pop them into his mouth without bothering. The salty fish tasted of the sea, and perhaps that is why Visko savored them so much.

Besides net-fishing with his father Ilija, they would also put out long baited lines from the shore. The lead weights kept the hooked ropes low in the water, and several hours later Visko pulled in moray eels, sea bass, and large octopuses. Bringing in the catch was always exciting for young Visko, as it was always a surprise what would be hooked to the line. And it was a whole lot easier than holding that boat steady for his papa!

Six days a week, life in the Njiric household was consumed by fishing and working on the farm. Every afternoon when they weren't fishing, Ilija or Franica had their children at the farm on the mountain behind their home helping them. There was much to do and the Njiric children grew up working hard. School, when they went, was only half a day, and after lunch and the afternoon nap that all the villagers took during the heat of mid-day, Visko and his sisters followed their parents to the farm. Depending on the time of year, there were olive trees and grapevines to prune and the fruit to pick, as the Njirics made their own olive oil and wine to use and sell. The gardens needed watering, which involved carrying buckets of water up the hill, and there was the constant need for wood to be gathered for Franica's cookstove. Visko would pull bunches of grass that grew between rocks on the steep hillside, stuffing them in a bag and emptying the full bags by laying them out to dry in the sun before stacking the dried grass piles up against a tree trunk to be used as hay for the animals.

Since Visko's daily chore was to walk the livestock the two or three miles up the mountain to the farm and bring them back down each day, he knew their ways better than anyone. The docile milk cow walked slowly and steadily behind his lead, but the goat wasn't always so cooperative and sometimes fought against the rope leading her when she'd rather be scampering amongst the rocks. Twice a day they gave their milk, most of which Franica used to make cheese. The sheep and occasionally the donkey followed Visko without a rope at all as they made their daily treks up and down the steep rocky path. Visko learned early in life that one never came down from the farm without carrying something back. Even if it was just a few sticks of wood on his shoulder, he never returned home empty-handed.

In a rock pit beside their home, the Njirics would raise a hog or two to butcher. When hog-killing time rolled around, Ilija enlisted the help of the whole neighborhood family. Every part of the hog was used. After the men had thrust a knife deep into the hog's chest just behind its legs to kill it and the hog quit thrashing, the knife was pulled out and a pan was quickly put into place to catch all the warm blood, so Franica could make the delicacy of blood pudding for her family to eat. Once the hair was burned off and the hog's skin scraped, then the hog was gutted. Most of the internal organs were edible, but even those that weren't eaten were used. The hog's intestines were thoroughly washed out, later to be filled with sausage, and the cleaned pig bladder was coveted as the perfect storage pouch for the men's tobacco. Nothing was thrown away during a hog-butchering.

Monday through Saturday was filled with labor, either on the land or sea, from before sunrise until after sunset, when the Njirics would fall into their burlap-bag-mattressed beds bone-weary from the day. But Sundays were a different story, and Visko lived for Sunday.

Church was mandatory every Sunday morning for the Njiric family. One had to be really sick to even consider staying home from church. Ilija and Franica, as well as their four children Visko, Cicilija, Anita, and Marica, along with Grandma Njiric, all donned their one set of Sunday-best clothes and set out for church. Most Sundays they would climb into the boat for Ilija to row them the short trip across the bay. But on occasions when the water was rough and choppy, they had to instead walk six miles or so along the shoreline to the big Catholic Church in Zaton Mali. Each person carrying his or her only pair of shoes, if indeed they even had any, the troupe walked barefoot to the church and then put their shoes on just before entering.

Being a Communist country, the Yugoslav government frowned on the devout Catholic church-going ways and religious traditions of the villagers, and the Party did its best to entice the youngsters away from Sunday morning services. Every Sunday morning just next to the church, the Communist Party would sponsor a free puppet show and invited the children to watch the show instead of going into the church. Ice cream and chocolate and candy would be served, rare treats for village children and even more so after the war. Every week Visko looked longingly at the puppet show and dared wish that he might be among the crowd of children sitting there waiting for it to begin, but when his step slowed even just a tad, he felt the nudging of Ilija and he reluctantly turned his head away from temptation and back toward the church doors. "Ice cream," Franica told him, "is made out of rotten eggs. You don't want to eat ice cream." As any child would, Visko believed his mother, and it wasn't until several years later after he had left home that a friend finally convinced Visko to at least try a bite of the cold creamy confection. All those years Franica had used that line to keep him and the other children from desiring a delicacy that they could not afford.

Franica and Grandma Njiric, dressed in black and wearing the required veils on their heads, reverently led the children down the center aisle to the front of the church where they would sit quietly together as Ilija took his seat with the other men in the back. Visko felt much more comfortable in his old worn clothes than the stiffly-pressed shirt and itchy wool shorts he wore on Sunday mornings, and he did his best to sit as quietly and still as possible lest his fidgeting and wiggling draw the inevitable stern warning look from Grandma's eyes. Some Sundays it seemed as if the service would never end, and Visko could hardly wait to peel out of his woolen Sunday clothes and free his brown toes from the tight leather hand-me-down shoes. When the last hymn had been sung and the final prayers recited, he could hardly get back up the aisle and out the big wooden doors fast enough. The family would visit with friends and neighbors for a few minutes before taking off their Sunday shoes and heading back home.

That's when the fun began. After the daily nap, it was play time! Sundays were days of relaxing and no work. Ilija wouldn't even shave that day nor allow Franica to do so much as pick up a needle on Sundays (although it seemed strange that he had no problem with her fixing family meals on the Sabbath).

For Visko and Branko and the other neighborhood cousins, it was a coveted free day. Most Sunday afternoons they headed down the hill to the seashore, where they loved to build sand mountains with roads and fashion animals out of old scraps of wire or anything else they might find. Splashing in the water together or racing to an anchored boat or diving for shells along the seafloor, the boys found plenty of fun in the simple playthings the seaside provided. Occasionally, Visko would leisurely swim the mile or so across the bay and lie in the sun for a while before swimming back home. The prospect of danger never occurred to these boys who had lived through a devastating and frightening war right there in their own village, and they played unchaperoned until they were forced inside by Sunday's setting sun.

The war had also brought a new selection of playthings for Visko and his friends. Undetonated German grenades were found scattered everywhere and, as most boys are, Visko was fascinated by the power contained inside that small can-shaped shell. On the bottom of each grenade was a long round wooden handle along with the detonating ring. After much experimentation and a few injury-causing mishaps, the lads discovered that grenades were great for fishing. Visko would hang onto the handle, pull the string and count "1, 2, 3," then throw the grenade into the middle of a school of fish in the water. The grenade exploded, causing a huge splash and killing all the fish which floated to the top of the water, and the boys would leap in with bags and collect them...a lot easier and quicker, plus a whole lot more fun than using a net, for sure!

Grenades added some extra excitement to the boys' Sunday afternoons. Just for fun, they'd pull the string and toss the grenades into the center of a group of rocks and watch them explode, laughing heartily as pieces of rocks flew high into the sky. Along with grenades, the Germans had also left strips of machine gun bullets, which Visko and his buddies would break apart and pour the gunpowder into an old can to keep for later use, perhaps to blow up an old stump or break apart a large rock.

Considering the dangerous nature of their newfound toys, injuries were not everyday occurrences, but those that did happen were on the serious side. In one mishap, Visko and Branko were both injured. Visko received a sizable chunk of shrapnel above his left eye when the boys unsuccessfully tried to pry open a stubborn bullet by taking a hammer to it, causing the whole thing to explode right in front of their faces. He tried to conceal the origin of his injury from his mother and grandmother, but the wound eventually became gangrenous, and he had to fess up, leading to a trip to the doctor's office to have the metal painfully removed. But boys will be boys, and even the occasional mishaps did not deter Visko and his friends.

Just past the Njiric house the Germans had dug three bunkers more than 20 feet deep, made of cement. Along the inside of the bunkers were built-in shelves and steps leading down to a huge treasure trove of explosives. At the bottom of the bunkers were bundles of TNT, each block about the size of a cake of soap, which the Germans had planned to use to blow up the road if necessary. As it happened, they never had the opportunity or need to do so and when the Nazi army left, it seemed they just left everything. The boys would climb down inside the bunkers, pull the fuses out of the dynamite packs, and bring the fuseless bundles out to use as fuel for fires. Without the fuse to ignite it, they found that the TNT wouldn't explode and made great fuel that burned much longer than a piece of wood. A can full of saltwater, a triangle of rocks to set it on, and some TNT lit underneath were all the boys needed to cook some of their freshly-caught fish.

Despite their poverty, life was good, and the Njirics knew no different. The ocean and land were generous to them, they worked hard, God blessed them with all they needed, and most of all they had each other. Visko loved his family and was a thriving lad there in Stikovica. In his ten short years on the earth and sea, Visko had already learned many lifetimes of lessons.

CHAPTER 8

Village Days

1949

Stikovica

Four years had passed since the Germans left, and slowly, steadily Stikovica was recovering.

In those four years, the Njiric family as well as all their neighbors and friends had labored long and hard to return life to normal. Just four years ago, Grandma Njiric and Franica had stood inside their ravaged seaside home with tears running down their cheeks, wondering how and if they would ever put their lives and home back together again. But if the war had taught them anything, it was resilience. The time for tears was over; it was time to get back to work.

The whitewashed lime-plaster walls, made fourteen inches thick to protect the home from being damaged by the frequent earthquakes, were bright again, and the sunlight bouncing off the sparkling turquoise sea waters and through the windows made the marble floors gleam. Wood was an expensive scarcity for building in Croatia, so much-more-affordable marble covered the floors instead. Delicious aromas were always wafting from the two kitchens, as

Grandma Njiric and Franica spent the better part of their days baking bread or making cheese or preparing meals for their ever-growing family.

Just below the dining room was an area carved out of stone, much like a root cellar, the size of a small room and about three feet deep, with the whole thing filled with olive oil that the Njiric family made from olives grown on their farm. A cool storage place for olive oil, it was also where the homemade cheese and even big fish were preserved. Wheels of cheese and fish like tuna were slipped into the oil, which sealed them and kept them from spoiling. Whenever Franica needed some oil, she would just dip out what she needed from the huge supply in that massive in-ground stone crock.

Fresh clean water was the one necessary commodity that was the hardest to come by. One would think living by the sea that water would be plentiful, but while saltwater was readily available there were some times of year that freshwater was not. The families depended on the rain to fill their cisterns, which kept them in water most of the year. Whatever rain did fall was caught off the roof and piped into a huge stone cistern on the lower level of the home. The family used this water for everything from cooking to bathing to watering the livestock and gardens. But during dry spells, Franica kept a watchful eye on the cistern, and when the water level dropped dangerously low another plan was put into action to refill the family's water supply.

Visko would climb down a ladder into the deep nearly-dry cistern, cleaning it out as best he could, grabbing with his quick hands the writhing eel that lived in the stone tank and putting him temporarily into a water-filled bucket. The mosquito-larvae-eating eel, as long as Visko was tall, provided the best water purification method they had available, and it worked quite well for them. After scrubbing down the cistern, it was time to scrub down the boat.

The inside of the boat, that is. Emptying it of the fishing net and other sundry items that accumulated over months of use, the innards of the wooden vessel were scrubbed and rinsed squeaky clean. Loading up a few empty water buckets, they tied the boat onto the back of another rowboat and headed across the bay to a nearby village where a freshwater spring flowed out of the ground. Visko helped his father and sisters fill buckets at the spring, carrying them down the hillside and dumping the fresh clean water into the freshly-scrubbed boat. Many, many trips up and down, back and forth, the crew carried dozens of buckets until the boat was full of spring water. Then Ilija would tow the water-filled boat home behind another rowboat where the bucket brigade began again, this time scooping water from the boat to carry and dump into the cistern to refill their water supply. Back and forth, back and forth, down to the sea and up the hill to their home, an exhausting all-day job for the Njiric clan. And when the huge stone reservoir was finally filled again, Visko caught the slippery eel and slipped him back into his cistern home.

Today the cistern was full and Visko didn't mind at all the chore of dipping out water. Bucket by bucket he carried it upstairs to the old kitchen, where he poured it into a big pot hanging over Grandma's fire pit. After a few trips, he got the tub and towels ready for bath time at the Njiric house.

Hot water was poured into the tub, mixed with just enough cold to make the water nice and warm. The whole family would share the tub of bath water before the evening was over. Three-year-old Marica was first, with Franica quickly scrubbing her little body before her seven-year-old sister Anita took her turn. Cicilija, now almost a young lady at ten, demanded privacy for her tub time and took a little longer than Visko thought necessary. He fiddled impatiently outside, wondering what was taking his sister so long. Normally, the weekly bath was not something Visko looked forward to, as he much preferred to consider his Adriatic Sea swims a satisfactory substitute for soap and warm water. But this week was different. Tomorrow was the big day that he, along with the whole village, had eagerly awaited for a whole year!

August 15 was, for every year that anyone could remember (excepting the war years when the village was occupied by Germans instead of Croatians), Stikovica's big festival, a holiday that everyone eagerly anticipated. Holidays were few and far between for the hard-working villagers, a day where no one worked and having fun was the only agenda for an entire day. Visko and his friends would spend the whole day mingling with the crowds in the streets, basking in the music and laughter, smelling the delicious aromas of vendors cooking food, just hanging around waiting for something exciting to happen. Even though he didn't have much money to spend, Visko's fingers felt the few coins jingling around in his pocket that he'd manage to convince Grandma to give him.

Grandma Njiric, as the eldest in the family, was the keeper of the purse strings. Any money that came into the household was immediately turned over to Grandma, and she doled it out miserly only as she saw fit. Since he'd turned eight years old, Visko had worked a couple of days each week in a tailor shop sewing buttons on shirts to earn a few pennies, pennies that went into Grandma's apron pocket. Countless times Visko had returned from the Dubrovnik market with his father and watched Ilija empty out his pockets of the profits they'd realized that day into the wrinkled hands of Grandma. She was the keeper of the family monies, and every penny that was spent came through her.

Visko, feeling quite manly now that he was eleven years old, smiled as he remembered the village festival last year. For a while, he'd taken fancy to a cute young village girl about his age. Although as a boy he was not allowed to play with girls other than his sisters, Visko had caught her eye a couple of times at school, and she'd flashed him her sweet smile. And Visko was pretty sure that when he'd gotten his palm whipped by the schoolteacher one day right before the summer holiday, he saw her out of the corner of his eye glance his way with big sad eyes, wincing as the switch came down. She liked him; he just knew it. Visko hadn't seen much of her all summer, but once in a while he'd catch a glimpse of her with her friends, their eyes meeting a few times, and Visko was pretty sure she smiled at him ever so slightly before turning back to her girlfriends.

Yes, she liked him. And Visko had decided just a year ago that he'd invite her to the big dance that capped off the village festival. Many years he'd sat with his friends in the packed dirt around the edge of the big oak tree in town, listening to the lively music and watching his neighbors laugh and whirl and kick up their heels, dancing until they'd kicked up a big cloud of dust all around them. He'd always wanted to join in the fun and last year, at the ripe old age of ten, Visko had been ready.

But first he had the daunting task of approaching Grandma for the money he needed to go to the dance. He figured ten cents would cover it... two cents each for them to get in, another two cents each for some lemonade, with two cents extra just in case he needed it. For a few days, Visko was on his very best behavior, strategically positioning himself into Grandma's good graces before he dared approach her with his request. He waited for just the right moment, and one afternoon when Grandma seemed to be in an unusually pleasant mood for some unknown reason, Visko took a deep breath and walked into the kitchen as Grandma was kneading bread on the table and asked her if he might have ten cents.

Looking up from her bread dough, Grandma's steely gaze met Visko's blue pleading eyes, and he quickly explained that he wanted to ask someone to the dance, and he figured five cents apiece would cover it. Then he held his breath as she stared through him for a moment or two. Visko felt confident that Grandma would give him five cents for his own admission, but he wasn't sure how she would react about his "date." After what seemed an eternity to a ten-year-old boy, Grandma brushed her hands together, dusting off the flour, and stuck her crinkled fingers into her apron pocket, counting out ten cents into Visko's palm.

"Thank you, Grandma!" Visko grinned at her and for the first time in a very long time, he was pretty sure that she was faintly smiling back at him.

What a great night that had been! His first dance, his first outing with a girl. Even though they were very closely chaperoned as their mothers sat on benches along the edge of the packed dirt circle keeping an eye on their every move, it had been a night Visko would never forget. And he hoped this festival, now that he was much more experienced at eleven years old, would be just as memorable.

This special holiday in August was one of the few opportunities Visko had all year to intermingle with girls. He found them strangely fascinating, not nearly as much fun as boys, but mysterious, and being around them made him feel all tingly. Recently he'd had his eye on a different village girl, a distant cousin of his, and he hoped he'd somehow get a chance to talk to her during the festival.

Visko and his friends meandered through the crowds all day long, and when night came the music grew louder and the dancing began in earnest. By this time, most of the villagers had consumed much more wine and beer than they wisely should have and the crowd noise was a little raucous at times. Visko kept an eye out for his new female interest, and when he spotted her alone along the edge of the crowd, he inconspicuously made his way her direction. Before the evening was over, Visko had kissed his first girl and went to bed later that night thinking he'd already gone to heaven, right there in the moonlight shining on Stikovica beside the Adriatic Sea.

CHAPTER 9

Dreaming of America

Summer of 1950

Stikovica

Stikovica and the neighboring villages were buzzing with excitement. If one paid no attention to the calendar, one might have believed a holiday was right around the corner. The air was pulsing with anticipation, people seeming a little happier and smiling a little easier.

Holidays had always been important events in Visko's life. Any day he got a break from farming and fishing was special, but holidays were times of long-held traditions and memory-making for the Njiric family.

Most were religious holidays, but the big fall Karneval was about as far from that as one might imagine. Visko was never quite sure how it originated and why the traditions were so crazy, but he had to admit it sure was a lot of fun, a celebration after the harvest and before the chilling winds of winter. A few days before the festival, the tradition called for every family to steal a donkey, although it was more accurately "borrowing" the donkeys, for after the ensuing parties were over, the donkeys were returned unharmed to their owners.

Visko loved that part of Karneval, and he put the cunning lessons he'd learned during the war into practice. To keep their donkeys safe from being taken, each family hid them in the best way they could, hoping to outwit the donkey thieves. One year Visko cleverly asked his uncle if he might borrow a gun and ammunition so he could go hunting. His uncle gladly obliged and Visko, who never had any intention of hunting at all, didn't bring home a single critter for dinner, but he did proudly trot his uncle's hidden long-eared four-hooved critter away from its mountain hiding place to be used in the festival parade.

And what a parade it was, a raucous, rowdy, drunken procession down Stikovica's gravel streets. The laughter began as the revelers fashioned a scarecrow-type dummy of sorts to sit atop the donkey, with a large empty goatskin and funnel on top where the head and chest should be. As the rabble roared with laughter down the dark streets, carrying torches to light the way, they would stop at each house where the villagers would pour a bottle or two of wine into the goatskin, gradually inflating it with the spirits. When the goatskin was full, the procession stopped at the edge of the village, built a big fire, and the partying began in earnest with plenty of drinking and dancing, singing and laughing…a good old time for everyone! As in most of Europe, children began drinking diluted wine as babies, so Visko and his friends joined in the rowdy celebration. Way past midnight, when all the wine was finally gone, the villagers stumbled back to their homes for a short night's sleep.

Then a couple of months later came Christmas, Visko's favorite holiday. Visko's mouth watered just thinking about all the edible delicacies that the family enjoyed only at Christmas, especially the roasted pig's head that his aunt prepared perfectly for the entire extended Njiric clan to feast upon after the midnight church service on Christmas Eve. All the way to the Catholic Church on the other side of the bay that night, Visko would walk with his family and neighbors through the darkness, pausing to sing Christmas carols in front of homes along the way, whose owners would open the door smiling and hand out candy to the children. Candy was a sweet treat that Visko very rarely saw, and he stashed his pockets full of as much candy as he could collect from the villagers. Christmas put everyone in a wonderfully happy state of mind, causing normally frugal folks to splurge on candies and such for the holiday.

Christmas gifts were meager, but indulgences just the same for the Njirics, often an apple or an orange, rare treats that Franica ordinarily would not give a second glance at the market. But Christmas was different, a time when hearts were softened and purse-strings were loosened. One especially memorable Christmas morning after the war, Visko awoke to the gift of a cap-gun while Cicilija received a doll, the only real toys Visko ever remembers them owning. But the coveted toys weren't for playing, as Grandma Njiric kept them in her dresser under lock and key, allowing them to be brought out only occasionally when special visitors called. Women came from miles around just to see the beautiful porcelain-faced doll that Cicilija, under the very watchful eye of Grandma, proudly displayed as the ladies cooed over and shyly touched the perfect creation. Visko's cap-gun roused the curiosity of the men and boys, but after a couple of quick demonstrations it was whisked out of his hands to be once more locked away with the precious doll until another special day.

There was one Christmas, though, that wasn't such a happy one for Visko. A couple of days before the holiday and the highly-anticipated huge family feast, Franica baked a lovely cake, placed it on a glass plate and covered it with a glass dome, putting the prepared cake on top of Grandma's dresser for safe-keeping until Christmas Day. Visko discovered the cake and decided that he MUST have a taste of it; he just couldn't wait until Christmas. So, he secretly climbed on a chair, lifted the glass dome, and ever-so-carefully tipped the cake sideways and carved out a small section from the middle underneath the cake. After tipping the cake back onto the plate, he was quite pleased with himself as the cake showed no signs at all of his tampering. Visko popped the morsel into his mouth, and the unfamiliar sweetness purely melted on his hungry little tongue. Try as he might, Visko couldn't get that heavenly taste out of his thoughts, and the next day he decided to get himself just one more little piece. Unfortunately for Visko though, Cicilija caught him in the act and threatened to tattle on him unless he gave her a piece too. And again, Visko carefully carved out another section, this time big enough for both of them to enjoy. As he placed the glass cover back into place, the cake looked fine, and Visko felt perhaps he had really gotten away with something.

Christmas Day all of the huge Njiric family gathered together at Tete Doma's (Ilija's sister) house for their traditional feast. As head of the family, Ilija had the honors of cutting the cake. Everyone watched as he removed the glass dome and stuck his knife into the cake, but to the great surprise of everyone else and to the horror of Visko, the middle of the cake completely collapsed, giving way to the hollowed out area underneath. All eyes were immediately turned upon Visko, the chief family mischief-maker, and that Christmas Day he got a whipping from Ilija that he never forgot.

Easter was a welcome holiday, ushering in the warmer breezes of spring as new life began to pop up in the fields and on the farm. The family celebrated the resurrection of God's Son at the Catholic Church that morning, followed by another big family meal together. Eggs were something Franica and Grandma rarely fixed, but on Easter they always boiled a batch for a special treat. Visko loved the game that he played with his cousins and uncles, throwing coins across the room at the hard-boiled eggs in a basket, slowly cracking and chipping away the hard shells. If he was lucky enough to make his coin stick into the solid egg white, Visko dashed across the room to retrieve his prize of that boiled egg to eat.

All of these holidays brought great joy to the hard-working villagers. But this time it wasn't a holiday spirit that was filling the village air with excitement. In some ways, the villagers were looking forward to an even bigger event, one that hadn't yet happened in the nearly five years since the war had ended. Stikovica was receiving a visitor from the other side of the world. Tete (*Aunt*) Eva, Franica's older sister, was arriving from California.

Visko was twelve years old now and, having completed the fourth grade just a few weeks before, he had finished his formal education. He'd learned how to read and write and figure numbers, about all the schooling he'd need to make his way in the world where he lived. There were fish to be caught and farming to do, and a twelve-year-old boy was needed to help bring money in to help support the family. He wasn't big in stature, but he was mighty in spirit, and Visko knew his responsibility well.

For weeks Visko had been helping Franica get ready for her sister's visit. The entire house was scrubbed top to bottom, the gardens weeded, and the flowers tended. Franica wanted everything to be just perfect when Eva arrived. Although they'd exchanged letters over the years, the sisters hadn't seen each other since years before the war, when Eva's husband had sent for her to join him in California. Leaving Croatia to make his fortune during the California Gold Rush in the late 1800's, he had later sent for his betrothed Eva to join him after he had gotten settled. The couple lived in California and were rearing their children there when Eva's husband met his untimely end in 1937, falling to his death while helping paint San Francisco's Golden Gate Bridge. Tete Eva had received a hefty insurance payment of $40,000 as a result of the accident, a huge amount of money in those days and certainly more than enough to provide for her and her two children, a daughter and a son, a very comfortable lifestyle. Soon after her first husband's death, she married a man who owned a large fleet of fishing boats. They weren't married long before he died, and since he had no family, Tete Eva inherited everything he owned. Not long after her second husband passed away, Tete Eva had married again, this time to a man much older than herself who was paralyzed due to a stroke and who was the landlord of several apartment houses in California. Just a few years later this third husband also died, and she acquired all of his assets as well, so by the time Tete Eva planned her 1950 visit to Yugoslavia, she was quite a rich woman, especially compared to her Croatian kinfolk back home.

If the Queen herself had been coming, the whole village couldn't have been more excited. Visko and his sisters had heard so many tales about Tete Eva and her unimaginable life in America that he could hardly wait to meet her in person. Ever since his encounter with the American sailors aboard the US destroyer just after the war, Visko's young mind had entertained the lingering dream to someday, somehow go to those United States, fueling his eagerness to find out from Tete Eva all he could about this seemingly Land of Opportunity where, as he fondly remembered, there was plenty of food for all.

Visko was quite curious about America, but even though he was twelve years old his knowledge about any country outside of Yugoslavia was extremely limited. Living in a tiny village in a Communist country, very little news leaked in from the outside world. Another of Visko's aunts, Ilija's sister Tete Maria, lived in New York City and occasionally the family would receive a letter with her return address, "New York, New York, USA." The few letters they did receive from Tete Maria and Tete Eva had already been opened by the government, so Visko's aunts knew they must keep their news general in nature and their opinions to themselves or the letters would never get past The Party authorities and into their family's hands. So news from America was nothing more than frivolous tidbits of information about his aunts' day-to-day life, nothing much of interest to a young boy like Visko.

The morning of her arrival, Visko joined his parents, sister, and a couple of their neighbors as they rowed three boats to Dubrovnik to meet Tete Eva at the seaport to bring her home. Eva had traveled with another Croatian woman cross-country from California to New York via train then cross-Atlantic aboard an ocean liner, a long journey that had taken a couple of weeks. Visko's heart was racing as they watched from the Dubrovnik shoreline as the huge ship approached. It seemed unbelievable that those people on board had sailed from the other side of the world, a world about which Visko had not an inkling. He watched mesmerized as the ship finally stopped and after what seemed like an eternity of waiting, passengers finally began to disembark.

Visko had no idea what Tete Eva looked like, but that didn't stop him from scanning every face, hoping to see one that looked like an older version of his mother. He glanced up at Franica's face, but her eyes were glued on the steady line of passengers. Suddenly a big smile broke across his mother's face, and she began waving frantically. Visko turned his gaze back toward the mob of strangers to see a fancy woman smiling and waving back. Tete Eva had arrived.

And she did not travel lightly. Visko couldn't believe his eyes as he and Ilija and their neighbors carried suitcase after suitcase, trunk after trunk from the luggage area on the dock to the three small rowboats. What could Tete Eva possibly have in all that baggage?! His whole life Visko only knew of his mother Franica having three dresses: one for church, one not quite as nice for visits to town or to wear temporarily while she washed her work dress, and one old one

*Dubrovnik,
Croatia*

photo by Zachary Nirich

for working. And Franica had only one pair of shoes, the pair she had worn in 1937 when she'd married Ilija. So surely there must be more than clothes in all those trunks. Visko thought it was a very good thing they had brought three boats to meet her, because by the time they had stacked all three of Tete Eva's trunks and the rest of her luggage into the boats, there was scarcely room left them to sit their bottoms down.

All the way back to Stikovica, Visko couldn't take his eyes off Tete Eva. She had a vaguely familiar resemblance to his mother and his Durovic grandparents, Grandma Ana and Grandpa Givo, but yet in many ways she looked nothing like them. Her hair was perfectly coifed under her elegant hat, and her lips and face were painted up as Visko had never seen on his mother or any other village women he knew. Tete Eva must have felt his blue eyes locked on her, as she turned her head to look back at this nephew of hers that she'd never met, forming those strangely bright red lips into a faint smile. Visko blushed and quickly smiled back before embarrassedly ducking his head, keeping his stares much stealthier the rest of the ride home.

Arriving at the Stikovica docks, Ilija and Franica helped Tete Eva get out of the rocking rowboat and gingerly make her way with her shiny high-heeled shoes up the path to the house. Visko enlisted the help of a few of his very curious cousin friends who were eager to catch a glimpse of this exotic stranger from another world, and they began unloading her luggage and hauling the heavy load up the hill, into the house, and upstairs to the bedroom that had been meticulously cleaned and prepared just for Tete Eva.

Visko never forgot the first time Franica sent him to Tete Eva's room to fetch her for breakfast the following morning. He timidly knocked on her closed door, shyly informing her that breakfast was ready if she'd like to join the family downstairs. When Tete Eva opened the door, Visko was stunned at the sight before him; blue dress, blue shoes, blue nylon-veiled hat, blue pocketbook, and adorned with blue jewelry around her neck and on her blue-gloved arms, Tete Eva was dressed completely in blue! Everything perfectly matched and coordinated, a creature the likes of which Visko had never before seen. Tete Eva confidently strode down the stairs with Visko sheepishly following behind her to the breakfast table. Visko could tell by the looks on his sisters' faces that they were just as shocked as he, and Franica ever-so-briefly caught her breath at the sight of her stylish but overdressed sister before smiling warmly and gesturing her toward her spot at the dining table. The four children could hardly eat between stealing glances at their aunt as Tete Eva seemed not to notice, primly and ever-so-properly eating her breakfast as they assumed was the delicate way of all American ladies.

Visko hadn't quite recovered from the mind-boggling sight of Tete Eva's impeccable breakfast ensemble when she appeared again for lunch...this time garbed from head to toe completely in pink. And then for dinner in green. Three totally different outfits in one day, and she hadn't lifted a soft, spoiled finger to soil any of them!

By the end of the first day of Tete Eva's visit, Visko had already made up his mind. He WAS going to America! He had no idea when or how, but someday, somehow he would live in that faraway place across the Atlantic where not only was food bountiful but people had more money than he ever dreamed possible in Yugoslavia. Visko's dream wasn't daunted by the fact that, since the war, the Communist government forbid anyone between the ages of six and sixty to leave the country. At twelve years old, Visko had no idea how he would make it happen, but he was convinced that someday, somehow he would live in the United States of America.

Tete Eva stayed several weeks with the Njiric family, during which time Visko plied her with questions about America whenever the opportunity arose. "How do people make money?" "What kinds of jobs are there?"

Tete Eva, amused at the interest of her young nephew, told him what he hoped to hear, that there were lots of jobs and money to be made, that anyone who was willing to work could earn a good living in America. Her words were encouraging, and the more Tete Eva told Visko the more determined he became that America was the place for him.

Despite her three trunks and assorted suitcases full of clothes, Tete Eva needed some new clothes to wear during her stay. Visko accompanied her into Dubrovnik for her shopping sprees, marveling at the seemingly endless supply of money to buy whatever her heart desired. One day, for no reason at all, Tete Eva just gave Visko three dollars. His eyes grew as big as saucers and, at least for the few hours he carried it in his pocket before turning it over to Grandma Njiric, Visko felt like a rich man. Tete Eva would always bring back from the city treats for the family, frivolous items that Franica would never dream of buying. Chocolate bars for the children, cigarettes for Ilija, and little gifts for her sister Franica... Tete Eva loved spending her money and the family loved it too.

All too soon it was time to say farewell to Tete Eva. Visko helped load her trunks and luggage onto the rowboats, and they accompanied her back to the port in Dubrovnik where she boarded a huge waiting ocean liner for her voyage back home. Hugging and kissing her family good-bye, Tete Eva waved her gloved hand at them as she walked toward the ship. Hers was a visit not soon forgotten by the villagers of Stikovica, a visit that changed Visko's life forever as it cemented in his mind his decision to go to the USA.

Visko didn't keep that decision a secret either. Every day he told Ilija his dream, that someday he was going to America. Ilija did not discourage him, but secretly believed it to be an impossibility. Visko was his only son, the heir to the Njiric property, and in his heart Ilija believed that as much as his twelve-year-old son dreamed of going to America, it was only a child's dream, and Visko would grow up to be a fisherman and farmer just like his father and grandfather before him.

Franica did, in fact, encourage her young son's harmless fantasies. "If that's what you want to do, it would be silly if you did NOT go," she'd tell Visko, even though she too doubted that he ever would. Dreams were a part of childhood, and God knows she'd had a few childhood dreams of her own. Let Visko fantasize about going to America now, for the realities of adulthood will hit him soon enough.

And dream, he did. Every day and every night Visko pondered about how his life might be someday in America. He was full of energy and willing to work, and Tete Eva had told him that was all it took to make money in America. Visko was only twelve years old, but as he closed his eyes to go to sleep each night on his lumpy burlap mattress, Visko knew in his heart that one morning someday he'd wake up far across the vast Atlantic Ocean in the country of his dreams.

CHAPTER 10

Sailing the Seas

1951

Adriatic Sea and beyond

A year had passed since Teta Eva's visit, but the sun had not set on a single day without Visko thinking about his future life in America. Thirteen years old now, he was indispensable to the Njiric family. Franica had just given birth to her fifth child, the pregnancy and birth being very difficult for her this time around, leaving her sick and weak. Finally another son, Ivo would be the last child for Ilija and Franica, and Ilija was proud of his new baby boy. But Ilija was also ailing, and it was getting harder and harder for him to earn enough money to provide for his family of six as well as his aging mother.

So when Visko approached his father about leaving home and joining the Merchant Marines to bring in some much-needed money for the family, Ilija agreed that it was a good idea. It would just be temporary, until Ilija got his strength back and was able to work again. Visko was thirteen now, old enough to be contributing to the family income.

The Njirics had a neighbor named Ivo, a man who worked on the ships as a Merchant Marine. Once when Ivo was home for a short leave to visit his wife and young children, Visko began hanging around asking him questions. Ivo told Visko about life on the ship; it was a good job where there was plenty to eat, and he was given clothes to wear. He told him that there was always a need for more people to work on the ships. The more Ivo talked, the more excited Visko got. Visko knew immediately that this was the perfect job for him, a job on the sea. And when he suggested it to Ilija, his father, even though cautioning that Visko had no idea what he was getting himself into, eventually agreed, so the two of them went into Dubrovnik to register Visko for service at the Merchant Marines office. He was issued a little card to keep, and every time they were in the city, Visko stopped by the agency to have his card dated and initialed again, keeping his name active on the recruit list.

Only thirteen years old, not quite five feet tall and weighing only 85 pounds, Visko was not exactly a prime candidate for the Merchant Marines. Besides that, normally to land a government position like the Merchant Marines, membership in the Communist Party would be required, even though at thirteen Visko was too young to join anyway. But had not Ilija used his considerable influence in the city, pulled a few strings, and delivered more than a few buckets of olive oil along with bottles of moonshine and wine to the right politicians, Visko would have never gotten a second glance. Despite all the strikes against him, counter-balanced by Puho's persuasive and considerable bribery, in July of 1951, after just a few months of impatiently waiting, Visko was offered a job working on the ships.

The morning Visko left, Ilija gave him three dollars to stash in his pocket as he bid his eldest son *bon voyage*. Visko was initially assigned to a ship that sailed back and forth through the Adriatic Sea, taking passengers as well as cargo to Italy and Albania and all the ports between, covering about a thousand miles of marine territory. With 110 islands in the Adriatic Sea and most having people living on them, there were lots of ports along that stretch of sea. For the first month of his Merchant Marine employment, Visko's ship cruised back and forth along the coastline, never too far from home, and when his ship ported in Dubrovnik about once a week, Ilija always made it a point to row over to the docks to see his son, sometimes bringing Franica along with him for a visit with their oldest child.

Life on board ship was even better than he expected. Visko shared a very small room in the belly of the ship with another young man, each of them sleeping in a flat bunk on chains that they folded down from the wall at night and pushed up during the day, so they could access the tiny closet where they kept their few possessions and ship-issued uniforms. Visko wore a cook's uniform, white pants with a checkered design with one of three shirt options, white, gray, or blue. Just outside their room and down the narrow steel hallway was a small bathroom that all the workers shared, with a shower room, sink, and commode. Having never enjoyed the luxury of indoor plumbing before, Visko felt he was living like a king aboard the ship!

Visko's position on the ship was that of a cook's helper, the lowliest of the kitchen workers. His first jobs were cleaning the pots and pans, sweeping and mopping the floor, and keeping the ship's kitchen in ship-shape. Being the small guy that he was, Visko wasn't able to reach over the edge of the big copper pots to scrub the bottoms clean, so he'd have to turn the pots onto their sides and crawl inside to finish washing them. The pots had to be so perfectly spotless and shiny that the cook could see his face reflected in them, and Visko worked diligently to be sure that was the case lest he have to rewash them until they passed inspection. Visko was the only cook's helper for three cooks, the First Cook, Second Cook, and Third Cook, who between the three of them kept him busy all day and sent him to his bunk exhausted every night. But, he wasn't complaining. At $14 per month that he never laid eyes on, as the only one in his family able to work at the time Visko was doing his duty. Whenever he was in Dubrovnik, Ilija would stop by the agency office and pick up the envelope with Visko's pay in it, enough to keep the Njiric family going for a little while longer.

Visko had only been serving on the Adriatic Sea ship for about a month when he was transferred to a different ship, this time one of the huge freighters that went overseas. Thrilled at the opportunity but nervous about being so far away from home, Visko was going to see the world! Up until now, he had very little knowledge of anything beyond the Adriatic Sea, and he was certainly up to the adventures that lay ahead.

The big overseas freighters had somewhere between forty-four and forty-eight crewmen on board, and Visko helped the cooks prepare three meals every day to serve to the Captain and all of his crew. The First Cook was a trained chef and made all the decisions regarding menus and such. At his orders, Visko would go down into the big walk-in refrigerator in the bottom of the ship, where it was the coolest, and bring up to the kitchen whatever meats and vegetables the chef needed for the day's meals.

Every morning Visko would get up at four o'clock to make coffee, taking the first cup of coffee up on the bridge to the Captain. After delivering coffee to the top officer on the ship, Visko began gathering together and readying all the ingredients for the breakfast meal. When the cook had the full-course breakfast prepared, the galley boy and the dining room boy would come down to the kitchen to get it and serve it to the officers and crew. Visko helped prepare the food and dished it out onto the plates but, as the kitchen boy, actually serving the meals was not part of his duties. On rare instances only did Visko ever take food to the dining room, perhaps if someone was eating at a different time than normal or on a special schedule. For the most part, he stayed in the kitchen doing the bidding of the cook, cleaning up and cooking.

Visko was used to working hard and he liked his job, which was certainly much easier than his fishing and farming life back in Stikovica. Even though he never saw his paycheck, he had everything he needed and the satisfaction of knowing that he was helping care for his family back home. Being gone for months at a time now, Visko rarely saw his loved ones once he began working on the overseas ships, but his mind's eye could see his father's smile of pride as he picked up Visko's wages each month in Dubrovnik, and at first, that was enough for Visko.

Until he found out about the black market. Visko hadn't been working long on the overseas ship when he began noticing unusual happenings and special caution being taken when the customs officers boarded the ships at port. The black market was something with which Visko was quite familiar, as his father Ilija had been involved in his own black market enterprises back in Yugoslavia as Visko was growing up. It didn't take Visko long to wise up and join in the black market schemes aboard ship, earning money of his own that he began to save.

Cigarettes were one of the main black market commodities. When the ship was docked in Gibraltar at the entrance to the Mediterranean Sea, Visko and his crewmates would buy American cigarettes for just eighty cents a carton, hide them aboard the ship, and then sell them for three dollars per carton (almost four times the original price) to dock workers when they ported in Italy. Visko had spent very little of the three dollars Ilija had given him when he left home, and he used the money to buy two or three cartons of cigarettes. Turning a big profit after selling them, he had more money to invest the next time around. And so it went, Visko making more and more money with each set of illicit transactions, money he used to buy his first new pair of shoes when he turned fourteen and other items that he wanted as the opportunities and desires presented themselves.

Black marketing was not without its risks and consequences, however. Each time the ship ported, customs officers from that country would board the ship and make inspections, looking for contraband merchandise. Visko got too greedy once, buying a whole case of cigarettes, 120 cartons instead of his normal dozen or so. Hiding a few cartons wasn't that difficult. Often Visko and the cooks, who were also doing black market trading themselves, would wrap bread dough around a box of cigarettes and put it in the loaf pan and into the oven during the inspections, fooling the customs officials into believing that they were just cooking loaves of bread. With the ovens big enough to hold about fifteen loaves of bread on each of two racks at a time, it was a simple effective solution to hiding thirty cartons of cigarettes. But concealing an entire case was another story. Visko attempted to disguise it in a corner of his room by covering it with blankets and clothes, trying to make the big box look like a dresser. The authorities weren't fooled and confiscated the whole case leaving Visko with a good tongue-lashing and nearly $100 lighter in contraband merchandise.

Later, when Visko traveled to far-away Asia on even bigger freighters, India was where Visko would get black peppercorns, paying fifty cents per kilo (about two pounds), which he later resold for five or six dollars in another country. Peppercorns were easy to hide, wrapping the package tightly in plastic and putting it at the bottom of a large trashcan, piling garbage on top of it only to dig it out after the customs officers had left. Another popular item that brought Visko a good profit was sunglasses, purchasing them in Portugal and Gibraltar and reselling them in Greece, Turkey, and other European countries. Occasionally, Visko would buy a tea set or two to resell. The good thing about smuggling tea sets was that if customs agents questioned him, he always told them he was bringing the tea sets back home to his family and they let it go. But the bad thing was that tea sets were not very profitable, only bringing in a couple of extra dollars, so most times they weren't worth the trouble.

Although the black market was illegal, it was not a secret and everyone working the docks at the ports, as well as the customs inspectors, knew it was going on right under their noses. The dock workers who boarded the ships to unload them would buy the contraband from Visko and the rest of the crew, then either resell or use it for themselves. Visko and his buddies found a pack of cigarettes to be more desirable currency than actual money when handed to a waitress at a restaurant while in port.

After World War II, many luxury items were hard to find and a lot of people profited from that fact, including many of the customs officials who were also crooked, all the while using their guise of government authority to cover their own black market running. The contraband items that they confiscated from inspecting ships were seldom if ever turned in, but instead resold by the officers themselves on the black market, lining their own pockets with great amounts of illegal money.

One day during mail call on the ship *Dubrovnik*, the freighter he was serving on at the time, Visko was handed a letter from his father. Pleasantly surprised, Visko ripped open the letter and began to read. Ilija wrote Visko that his sister Cicilija was about to get married, and the family needed the traditional gift of a sewing machine to present to her as part of her dowry on her wedding day. In Communist Yugoslavia, new sewing machines were very scarce and those few that were available were extremely expensive. Ilija was hoping Visko could help them obtain a sewing machine on his travels.

Wanting to help solve his father's dilemma but puzzled as to how he might possibly smuggle such a big heavy item back home, while he was on leave in Italy, Visko purchased a sewing machine for five dollars and hid it in his room. Knowing that the *Dubrovnik's* planned route would take them near Zaton Mali and in fact in sight of the Njiric home on their way to Rijeka, an Adriatic Sea port in the northern-most corner of Yugoslavia, Visko came up with a plan and wrote his father back with the details, telling Ilija the date and time to expect the *Dubrovnik* to pass by in front of Stikovica.

After wrapping the sewing machine securely in many, many layers of plastic, Visko questioned the sailor in charge of the deck and found out the water was 150 meters (about 450 feet) deep there in that area of the bay. Making sure he had plenty of rope, Visko tied the water-proofed machine onto one end and attached a wooden buoy to the other, and just as the ship passed in front of the Njiric house Visko tossed the plastic package, rope, and buoy overboard and watched as the sewing machine immediately disappeared out of sight sinking to the bottom of the bay leaving only the colorful buoy bobbing in the waves. As the ship steamed ahead, Visko soon lost sight of the small buoy and hoped his father had gotten his message. Indeed, Visko found out later, Ilija had and as soon as Ilija had spotted the *Dubrovnik* passing by, he rowed his own boat out into the bay, located the buoy, and hauled the sewing machine 450 feet up out of the sea and into his boat. That sewing machine was the largest and most complicated smuggling act Visko ever attempted, and he was quite proud that his scheme had unfolded exactly as planned.

Following his stint of service on the *Dubrovnik* which sailed in and around the Mediterranean Sea, over the next couple of years Visko was reassigned to even bigger freighters which ventured farther than Visko had ever even dreamed of going... South America, three or four trips on the *Drvar* to Singapore, Hong Kong, and Japan, to Burma and India several times, and many stops in Africa...exotic faraway places that were amazing different worlds to a teenage village boy from Croatia. Each voyage lasted for months with many ports, and occasionally when Egypt's Suez Canal was closed due to warring in the area, the ships would have to go all the way around the southern tip of the continent of Africa, essentially doubling their time at sea. Passing through the waters of the earth's equator, the extreme and nearly unbearable scorching heat made the ship's metal decks so blisteringly hot that the sailors continually sprayed water across the steaming steel in an attempt to keep the decks cool enough to walk across, and Visko and his friends wondered how anyone on earth was able to survive such torrid temperatures.

So many ships and so many ports, after a while they all began to meld together, and later as he tried to recall those years Visko had trouble remembering which ship had gone where.

CHAPTER 11

Ocean Calamity

Winter 1955

Indian Ocean

A Second Cook by now, Visko had climbed the ranks of kitchen help over the past three years, at the age of seventeen an accomplished cook in his own right. This first voyage on his newly assigned freighter was especially exciting. Sailing toward China in the late summer of 1955, this ship carrying a load of rice would be the first cargo ship from any European country to go to China in the ten years since World War II had ended. Visko had no idea at the time, but his first trip to China would also be his last.

Winter had arrived by the time the huge freighter finally neared the port at Qinhuangdao on the northern shore of China's Yellow Sea. The bitter wind chilled Visko and his crewmates to the bone, and the unusually frigid temperatures froze the waters around the ship before it could even reach the shore, locking the massive steel hulk in the ice. Try as they might, the crew was not able to free the freighter from the water's frozen grip and they found themselves stuck.

Visko watched from high on the deck as a long, straight stream of Chinese workers, even in the brutally treacherous weather conditions, walked about a quarter mile across the frozen sea from the shore, boarded the ship, and carried the bags of rice in a steady line off the ship until it was completely unloaded. Visko grinned as he watched them from afar, thinking they looked much like a scene from his childhood, like hundreds of ants following each other single file and carrying food on their shoulders, very organized and almost mechanical in their movements.

Emptying the ship of its cargo lightened the freighter, but it still wouldn't budge from the ice. There was nothing else to do but wait for an icebreaker ship to arrive and free them. With the outside temperature at about -40 degrees Fahrenheit, it wasn't long before all the men on the ship were freezing. They had no clothing suited for such extreme cold, and since the ship's generator required flowing water to keep it running, they weren't able to use it and had no power on the ship. Without power there was no heat and no way to cook, leaving the kitchen crew to provide meals the best they could. At night, the seamen bundled up in layers of clothing and blankets to sleep on the ship, but during the day they usually got off.

The Chinese people were very kind to the stranded men, giving them insulated coveralls, gloves, and hats to keep them warm and feeding them some hot meals as well. A couple of mini-buses would pick the crew up at the shore in the morning and chauffeur them around to various places to fill the days. Visko was awestruck to see the Great Wall of China, a wonder of the world that he never even knew existed, and the landscapes between Mongolia and China were unlike any he'd ever seen. The crew was thankful for a Chinese man that served as interpreter for them, translating the Chinese words into English for one of the ship's crewmen to further translate into Croatian so Visko and his friends could understand. One day the seamen were treated to a variety show complete with costumes, dancing, and singing put on by their newfound friends. Visko was thrilled to find out that they were even scheduled to have an audience with the Emperor of China in a few days! The Chinese people demonstrated great hospitality and generosity to their fellow

Communists brothers during their stay.

Finally after two weeks in China, and the very morning that the men were scheduled to go see the Emperor in his palace, the icebreaker arrived, freeing the ice-bound ship and disappointedly canceling the crew's much-anticipated imperial visit. After thanking the Chinese friends for their kindness, the freighter steamed out of the Yellow Sea and southwestward toward home.

But their voyage home proved to be quite calamitous for the freighter. Unbeknownst to the crew, over the course of the ship's two-week frozen imprisonment that expanding ice had weakened the empty ship's welded seams and perhaps even caused the beginnings of cracks that would eventually put the ship and its crew in deep peril.

The crew knew nothing of the problems in the belly of the ship when they ported at the island of Formosa. From there they went to Hong Kong, picking up cargo in the form of huge shipping crates at each place before pointing the ship's prow toward Italy. They had a few days of smooth sailing before they found themselves in the middle of a typhoon, high winds and torrential rains pounding the ship and tossing it around the mighty Indian Ocean like a child's tiny toy. Visko had seen many storms in his years with the Merchant Marines, but nothing to compare with this monster, and although none of the men were eager to admit it they were all scared for their lives.

Only adding to their terror was the report from the crewman responsible for regularly checking the boat's safety that a metal seam had cracked and water was leaking into the hull. Hard as they worked, the ship's pumps could not keep up with the water pouring in and eventually the sturdy vessel, weakened from being squeezed by the ice, cracked down the middle and the rear of the ship began to tilt into the water. Despite the efforts of the one welder on board to fix the leak, water continued to pour into the ship's belly, and the Captain ordered all the crew up on the very top of the ship as their rooms below slowly filled with water. Visko and his crewmates huddled against the storm on the bridge with the Captain, helplessly watching their ship sink lower and lower into the raging sea until only about fifteen feet was left above water, the bridge and the arms. Thankfully, when the storm abated the cracked area was above the water line stopping the leakage, but the ship was seriously damaged. The Captain warned what they all knew, that if what remained of the boat itself began tipping to the side, there would be no saving it. Or them...although the Captain didn't say that, they all knew the truth that there was a very good chance that all of them could soon end up at the bottom of the ocean.

To say Visko was frightened was an understatement. He couldn't help but wonder that perhaps he would never see his eighteenth birthday. He was scared, more scared than he'd ever been in his life. One morning as the light was dawning one of his shipmates noticed a stark white shock of hair about the size of a quarter had appeared overnight in the thick dark hair falling across Visko's forehead. Apparently caused by the extreme stress Visko was under, for the rest of his days every time he looked in a mirror that patch of white hair would forever remind Visko of those harrowing days on that crippled ship.

But as terrified as he was, somehow deep in his heart Visko knew that an ocean grave was not his destiny. He had his sights set on America and a dream to yet fulfill. As Visko saw it, the sea, which had given him birth and provided him joy and sustenance for all his days, was a giver of life not death. So, he diligently prayed and kept strong in his faith as the ship struggled on, critically wounded but still puttering upright through the briny waves, around the tip of Africa, and finally the seamen all breathed a collective sigh of relief and thanksgiving as the ship limped into the harbor at Naples, Italy. Visko, as much as he loved the sea, had never been happier to set his feet down onto solid ground.

After the cargo, much of it damaged by the seawater, was

unloaded, the Captain met with his officers and crew. Having traveled as far as it could and much farther than it should have, the ship was put into dry dock in Naples for repairs leaving 46 men temporarily unemployed and homeless. Since no one could live on the ship for the estimated 30-60 days it was to be in dry dock, Visko and the others were given three choices: stay in a hotel, be placed for temporary duty on another ship, or go home on leave while the ship was being repaired. Visko, still feeling himself very fortunate to have survived his last voyage, as well as the fact that it had been quite a long time since he'd seen his family, quickly decided on the third option. He would go home.

The Captain, however, thought Visko might be enticed to serve on another ship when he shared the details. A luxury Italian ocean liner, a huge passenger ship called the *Andrea Doria* was in need of a baker. "No," Visko said. "I think I'll go home." But when the Captain threw in the fact that the pay was $30 a month, double what he had been making before, Visko quickly changed his mind. And so Visko was temporarily reassigned in March of 1956 to serve as a baker, working daily from six o'clock at night until six in the morning, on the famous *Andrea Doria*.

CHAPTER 12

Aboard the *Andrea Doria*

Late March 1956

The Atlantic Ocean

Visko could hardly believe his eyes as he walked onto the *Andrea Doria*. He'd been on many sea vessels in his eighteen years, but this ship was unlike any he had ever seen. Gorgeous hand-painted murals adorned the walls, graceful white columns marked the hallways, lavish carpeting and wall-coverings surrounded him. The chatter and laughter of wealthy travelers filled the air. Visko was in another world.

Launched from Genoa, Italy and the namesake of one of Genoa's most famous admirals, the *Andrea Doria* was Italy's pride of the seas. Built for beauty and luxury, over one million American dollars had been spent purely on her decor and included numerous expensive artworks, including a full-size sculpture of Admiral Doria. Her staterooms were state-of-the art with private bathrooms, and the entire passenger area of the ship was air-conditioned. She was the only ship at the time to boast of three outdoor swimming pools. Visko was amazed at the design of the elegant dining room, engineered to rest on ball bearings so that the floor absorbed the movement of the waves and always remained level. She may not have been the largest or the fastest, but the *Andrea Doria* was without a doubt one of the most beautiful and safest ships to have ever sailed the seas.

Feeling like a servant in a palace, Visko knew right away he'd made the right decision when he took his captain's offer to work a few weeks aboard the *Andrea Doria.* He settled into his new room, hardly believing his good fortune at landing a job aboard this fabulous ship. He was a baker, beginning his shift at six o'clock each evening and baking bread and pastries all night long while the rest of the ship slept, finally falling into his bunk after he finished his night's work at six o'clock in the morning. With a capacity of approximately 1240 passengers and 560 crew members, there were lots of mouths to feed during the ten-day ocean crossing.

To say that Visko was elated when he discovered that the ship was sailing toward America was an understatement, to say the least. In the nearly eleven years that had passed since Visko had filled his starving tummy aboard the US destroyer sitting in Zaton Mali Bay, rarely had a day gone by that Visko hadn't thought of his promise to himself that one day he would go to America. And now, here he was, just a few days away from seeing for himself the country of his dreams! Scheduled to port in New York City the first week of April, Visko would have a chance to take his day's leave to get off the ship and explore for himself.

Lying in his bunk one morning just after waking, the idea suddenly occurred to Visko. This was his chance, the one he'd been living for the past eleven years! His mind racing as he lay there quietly, listening to the steady hum of the ship steaming ever closer to New York, he formulated his plan. Yes, he could do this! He would jump ship and begin his life in America!!!

The next few days crept along, as Visko could hardly contain his excitement. Of course, he hadn't breathed a word to anyone about his plans. He did, however, put in a request for two days' leave instead of the normal one day, telling his superiors truthfully that he had an aunt and uncle in New York City, and he'd like the chance to visit with them while he was there. His request was granted and, carefully and secretly, knowing his scheme was very risky and illegal on several counts, Visko calculated his departure from the *Andrea Doria*. This was the opportunity he had hoped for, prayed about, and counted on his whole life, and he was not about to let it slip through his fingers.

As the *Andrea Doria* eased into the New York harbor, Visko craned to see this city he had dreamed about for so long, and he couldn't believe all the vehicles he saw...cars, buses, trucks, taxi cabs, vehicles of every kind, color, and size EVERYWHERE! In all his imaginings of New York City, Visko had assumed it must be much like the largest city he'd ever seen, Dubrovnik. But in Dubrovnik, the only vehicle one might occasionally see was a delivery truck or the city's lone taxi cab. People used bicycles, donkey carts, and mostly walking to maneuver around the city. He didn't realize there could be that many cars in the entire world, and all he could assume was that there must be a big meeting in New York City of everyone in the whole United States to account for so many vehicles in the streets. He watched as the passengers disembarked, longing for his own opportunity. But before he would be allowed his two-day leave, Visko had another day on the *Andrea Doria*.

After unloading all the passengers and their luggage, immigration officials came on board and issued all of the crew passes. Visko looked at the card he was handed: Visko Ivo Njiric, 6 February, 1938, Yugoslavia, *Andrea Doria*. With the official business paperwork completed, the beautiful ocean liner slowly backed out of the harbor and made its way up the Hudson River to Albany, New York to pick up provisions for her return voyage to Europe. Visko peered out the porthole every chance he got, eager to see as much as possible of this new land that he would soon call "home." The river was beautiful, banked with trees broken up many times by what he assumed to be villages along the way. Arriving in Albany, when the ship had been restocked, Visko, nervous but trying his best to hide his excitement, was permitted to get off.

So with just the clothes on his back (his ship-issued black pants and shirt, and a sports coat), a few American dollars in his pocket, his identification card, and the phrase "I am hungry" being the only English he spoke, on April 6, 1956 with his heart pounding, Visko did not even glance back as he walked down the gangplank and off the *Andrea Doria* into his new American life.

CHAPTER 13

AMERICA!

April 6, 1956

New York City

Standing on the sidewalk with his hands shoved into his pockets, Visko looked all around him in amazement. He'd sailed the globe many times, but all his travels didn't begin to prepare him for what he saw. Never in his wildest imaginings had he ever envisioned America to be so busy! Cars honked all around him, buses whizzed by, strange odors puzzled his nose, and a cacophony of foreign sounds deafened him. It was a whole new world, a world where Visko was an alien. Yes, he was a little scared, but even in his fear of this unknown new world, Visko was never daunted. Somehow he would find Dundo (*Uncle*) Niko in this vast sea of people and Dundo Niko would help him get his feet planted in America.

A crew member from the *Andrea Doria* who spoke both Croatian and English hailed Visko a cab, giving the driver instructions to take Visko to the train station and help him get a train ticket to New York City. After paying the taxi driver three dollars (including the tip, as his fellow seaman had informed him to do), Visko went to the ticket booth, paid his fare, and boarded the next train bound for Grand Central Station in the heart of New York City.

The train seemed to fly down the tracks, bombarding and dizzying Visko with buildings and cars and crowds of people blurring past the windows. As the railroad tracks followed alongside the Hudson River, his seat aboard the train provided a beautiful view of the river as well. Seated around Visko inside the passenger car, he saw businessmen reading newspapers, others staring blankly out the windows, women clutching their purses and bobbing back and forth with the train's rocking movement. People were babbling in strange languages, none of which made any sense to Visko's ears. Looking around him, there were Negros and Asians, people whose skin were white and black and every color in between, poor and rich, male and female, such an ethnic assortment of humankind all in one place. He clutched his seat and looked back out the window, steadying himself as his senses were overloaded as never before in his eighteen years.

At each station stop Visko watched the other passengers, wondering if this was where he should get off. A few boarded and a few left, so Visko followed his instincts and stayed put, remembering the advice of the Croatian man who had hailed his cab, "When everybody gets off, you get off too." That's how he'd know when he reached New York City.

And that he did. When the train screeched to a quivering halt in what he learned later was Grand Central Station, the mass of people shoved Visko aside to push out the open train door. Visko shrunk against the inside of the car until it was nearly empty, then took a deep breath and stepped off the train.

People, people, PEOPLE EVERYWHERE..... a strangely-organized horde of men, women, and a few children walking back and forth across in front of him. Visko stepped into the moving stream of bodies, being swept along in the flow. Restaurants, newsstands, stores... so this must be New York City!

But the more he looked around, the more Visko became confused. Where were all the cars he'd seen from the ship and train? All he saw here were trains and business establishments and people, lots and lots and lots of people. He wandered around a few minutes, turning his head back and forth in a futile attempt to take in everything around him. Then he looked up. No sky! And suddenly he realized why, despite the electrical lights, it seemed so dim and dark. He was underground in the biggest tunnel he had ever seen!

Visko walked and walked for what seemed like miles and hours, but he couldn't find a way out of the maze. How was he going to get out of there?! There had to be a way to get up and out because Visko knew that everyone surely didn't live underground. As he pondered his predicament, he noticed a man with a briefcase striding confidently across his path, and Visko decided to follow the man. Surely, the man would eventually lead him outside into the REAL city. As the man in the black hat weaved his way through the human horde, Visko wasn't far behind. When the man stopped at what Visko realized later was a telephone booth, Visko stopped too, and as the man was talking on the telephone, Visko noticed there was a stairway nearby, so up the stairs he went, blinking and smiling into the bright spring sunshine.

While aboard the ship, Visko had heard some advice that he never forgot. During a staff briefing about what one could expect in New York City, the crew was told that if they ever got lost in New York City to go to the big Catholic Church on the corner of 8th Avenue and 50th Street, and right next to that church was a bar. The church and the bar were both Croatian and someone in one or the other would surely be able to help.

So that's what Visko set out to do. He was, after all, good with numbers and surely he could find 8th and 50th. Walking the crowded sidewalks on the hot spring day, Visko looked at the street signs at each corner, determining whether the street numbers were getting bigger or smaller. Eventually, after a couple of hours and thirty or forty blocks worth of walking, Visko found the church and bar. Quite proud of himself for getting this far, Visko looked around for someone to help him but then became doubtful that this indeed was the right church after all. The signs were in English, not Croatian. Puzzled about what to do, Visko reasoned that perhaps he hadn't remembered the correct address at all, so he kept on walking along 50th Street and the numbers of the avenues continued getting lower. He knew that the closer he was to the harbor, the smaller the numbers would be, and by the time he reached 3rd Avenue about 3:00 that afternoon Visko was hot, tired, confused, and famished.

Glancing around at the building behind him, Visko saw a set of double swinging doors that had been propped open in the heat of the day, and he walked through them, climbed three stairs, stepped into the smoky dimness, and sat down at the counter of a bar. His legs were exhausted, and it felt so good just to sit down for a moment to get his bearings. Meeting him at the other side of the bar counter, the bartender asked him, "What do you want?"

Visko, not understanding a single word that the man had said, spoke the only English phrase he knew. "I am hungry."

"What do you want to eat?" the man asked him.

"I am hungry," Visko replied, knowing nothing else to say.

"Do you want a sandwich?" As Visko shrugged his shoulders and gestured with his hands, the bartender soon realized that this young man sitting in front of him couldn't speak English, and he disappeared into the back.

Reappearing in a few minutes with a ham and cheese sandwich on a plate, he set it in front of the grinning Visko. Feeling a little more confident now and using his hands to act it out, Visko asked, "Pivo?" as he ordered a beer.

"How old are you?" the bartender asked. Not understanding the question, Visko shrugged his shoulders again. Attempting to help him understand, the man demonstrated by pulling out his wallet and showing Visko his driver's license. Visko realized what the man wanted, so he stood up and dug into his own pockets, pulling out his

ID card that the immigration officials had given him when he left the *Andrea Doria* and handing it over to the bartender.

Legal drinking age in New York at that time was eighteen years old, so after checking his ID and seeing that Visko had indeed turned eighteen a couple of months earlier, the man brought him a beer. Never had a mug of beer looked so refreshing before! As Visko picked up the frosty glass and began thirstily drinking, the bartender held up his finger. "One moment," he said, and Visko watched as the man picked up the telephone and began talking to someone.

With a sandwich in one hand and a beer in the other, Visko was feeling much better already. Before he'd even finished his sandwich, another man walked through the open double doors, stopped next to Visko, and shocked Visko by greeting him in Croatian.

Someone who could understand him! Visko was overcome with relief that finally he'd be able to communicate. The bartender, seeing from Visko's card that he was from Yugoslavia, had called a Croatian friend of his who lived nearby to come and help.

Visko told the Croatian man that he had an aunt and uncle who lived someplace in New York, and he wanted to find them. Visko knew that if only he could go see Tete Maria and Dundo Niko that they would help him get settled into his new life. But he had no idea where to even begin searching... the only address he'd ever noticed on Tete Maria's occasional letters to her sister Franica was "New York, New York," and it hadn't taken Visko long to realize that he could do a whole lifetime of searching in this huge metropolis and perhaps never even come close to finding them on his own.

"Do you have your uncle's telephone number?" the man asked him.

"No."

"What about their address? Do you know their address?"

"No." This was going nowhere fast. "But I do know his name," Visko replied.

"I sure hope it's not Smith or Jones," the man grinned. Visko had no idea why that was so funny, but he grinned too.

"Vodopia. My uncle's last name is Vodopia."

Reaching below the counter, the bartender pulled out a stack of thick dirtied, yellowed books. Phone books they were, one for Queens, one for the Bronx, one for Brooklyn, one for Manhattan, one for Staten Island, several phone books all big and thick. And, as the three men began paging through them one by one, Visko soon understood and was indeed thankful himself that his uncle's name was not Smith or Jones. So many people! Each name in those heavy thick books represented a whole family! The very thought boggled Visko's mind.

The first three books yielded nothing. The man called a couple of phone numbers belonging to someone whose name was close to Vodopia, but in typical New York fashion the voices on the other end of the line hung up on him. Finally, in the book with the big black letters "Queens" on the front, way back in the "V" section they spotted it.

Niko Vodopia.

That had to be him. Dundo Niko.

One of the men dialed the listed number and handed the telephone to Visko. The black receiver felt heavy in his hands and, with butterflies in his stomach, Visko held it up against his ear and nervously listened to the buzzing as the phone was ringing in what he hoped was his uncle's home somewhere in the New York City borough of Queens.

"Hello?" a female voice spoke through the wires. Tete Maria had answered the phone since her husband Niko wasn't yet home from work. Hearing nothing but silence for a few seconds, she repeated, "Hello?"

Fearing she might hang up if he didn't speak quickly, Visko responded in Croatian, "Hello. My name is Visko Njiric, your nephew from Yugoslavia. I am in New York City and wondered if Dundo Niko might come pick me up."

Stunned, Tete Maria didn't quite know what to say. She couldn't believe what she was hearing. Her nephew, Ilija's eldest, here from Yugoslavia? She explained that Niko was still at work but should be home in a few minutes.

"Does Dundo Niko have a car?"

"Oh, yes," Tete Maria answered in their native tongue. "Niko has a car and as soon as he gets home I will send him to pick you up. You stay right where you are, and Niko will come to get you as soon as he can."

Visko handed the phone back to the bartender, who gave Tete Maria the address of the bar, thanked her, and then hung up the telephone. "Wait right there," she had told him. So wait Visko did, and about an hour later Dundo Niko strode into the bar and, spotting his nephew right away, the two exchanged excited hugs and the traditional cheek kisses.

Dundo Niko shook hands with the bartender and his helpful Croatian friend, and Visko did the same. Following Dundo Niko down the steps and out the doors, onto the sidewalk and into his car, Visko finally felt himself beginning to breathe normally again. After over a decade of dreaming about going to America, he had finally made it happen. He was in America... he was home.

CHAPTER 14

Getting Settled

Spring 1956

Flushing, New York

Tete Maria was watching out the window when the car
pulled in the driveway, and she hurried outside to greet
her husband Niko and Visko. Back in the late 1800's, Niko had left
Old Croatia to come to the United States for work and make a living,
settling in New York and getting his citizenship papers, then sending
for Maria, Ilija's sister, to join him.

Niko and Maria had made a good life for themselves here in
America where they'd raised their two sons. Maria was proud of
their home, modest but comfortable, and Niko's hard work had paid
off for them. Her children were now grown; she was even a
grandmother, and so pleased that one of their sons, Nick, and his wife
had their own apartment on the upper level of their home. They had
given Niko and Maria two beautiful grandchildren. Life was good,
and they were happy in their Flushing, New York neighborhood.

As thrilled as Tete Maria was to finally meet her nephew and
hear first-hand news from her family back in Yugoslavia, her smile
faded and her bright eyes dimmed when she heard his story. Visko
wasn't there just for a visit. He intended to stay, and he hoped to live

with them for a while.

It wasn't that Visko wasn't welcome. He was. Family helped family; it was the Croatian way. What worried Maria was the fact that Visko was in America illegally. All these years she had lived in the US, Maria had never felt the need to learn the language and was only a citizen through her marriage to Niko. She feared that by harboring Visko they'd all get in trouble. Maria couldn't bear the thought that perhaps the government might even deport her. So even though Visko was family and as much as she wanted to help him, she couldn't. She just wouldn't allow him to live with her and Niko.

"Oh, no, no, no. You can't stay with us," Tete Maria admonished, her fearful, pleading eyes looking up at her husband. "You must find your own place. You can't live here. We'll all get in trouble!"

Visko's cousin Nick spoke up. "Come live with us," he offered. "I'm not afraid of the immigration officials. They can't deport me. I was born here in the United States, a natural-born US citizen and an ex-Marine. They wouldn't dare try to deport me."

So Tete Maria reluctantly agreed, and Visko moved into the upstairs apartment with his cousin Nick, his wife, and their two young children in a small neighborhood in the suburban city of Flushing, New York.

Visko was happy to have found a place to lay his head, but he was eager to get to work. He'd come here to make his fortune, to live the American dream, to use his youthful energy and enthusiasm to build his own life here in the US. Hard work and long hours did not scare Visko. He'd done both his whole life. But this time it was for himself, not for his family. He was a man now and he was eager to get started on his own American dream.

He'd only been at Nick's for a few days when Visko's first job opportunity presented itself. Just a few houses down the street, on the same block as the Vodopias, lived Nick's in-laws. His father-in-law had been having trouble with a low area in the front yard of their home where the dirt seemed to be continually sinking down, and he couldn't figure out why. So, Nick's father-in-law asked Visko if he might dig it out and try to fix it, and he would pay him for the work.

Visko could hardly contain his excitement. His first job! Of course, he would! Very early the next morning, as soon as it was daylight, Visko borrowed Dundo Niko's shovel and pick, put them on his shoulder, and bounced down the sidewalk, eager to get started. As he was digging, people began leaning out windows and yelling at him. Not understanding what or why they were yelling, Visko was puzzled but just waved and smiled back at them and kept right on digging. Later, as he was asking Nick why the neighbors had been upset, Visko discovered that apparently in American cities and especially on Saturday mornings people don't start working quite so early, and he was waking them. Americans have strange ways, Visko thought, still sleeping after the sun had risen.

It didn't take long for Visko to discover the problem. Underground in Nick's father-in-law's front yard there was an old cistern that had not been filled in properly when it was no longer used, and a broken plumbing pipe was causing water to seep into the well and the dirt to continually sink in around it. When Nick came home from work, Visko showed him the problem and the two of them went to the store, bought some concrete mix and a new pipe, and together they fixed the problem. Visko covered the hole back up; the project was finished in one day. When Nick's father-in-law handed Visko a twenty-dollar bill, the young man couldn't believe his fortune. Visko thought he was the richest man in the world, making twenty dollars for one day's work when he'd had to work a whole month in the Merchant Marines just to earn fourteen dollars that he'd never even seen. It was the first money Visko had ever made besides his black market money on the boat, this money earned with the hard work of his hands. What Tete Eva had told him when she'd visited Stikovica six years ago was true. America truly was the land of opportunity!

CHAPTER 15

New Name, New Life

Summer 1956

New York City

Staring up at the clear night sky just outside the Vodopia home, Visko felt at peace. He'd always loved gazing at the stars, amazed at the magnificence and vastness of God's creation, and incredulous that those same stars that he was gazing at here in his new American home were the very same sky lights that had awed him as a child.

Visko knew the constellations well and could quickly spot them. His father had even taught him how to navigate the seas like his ancient mariner ancestors had so long ago, sailing boats through the night with only the stars to guide them. Those same stars Visko was looking at in wonderment this very moment had been his constant friends his whole life. Sleeping on the hard cold earth as a young scared boy during his war-time forages, the stars overhead had comforted him. They'd lit the boat's path during the dark mornings when he and his father had rowed across the black waters to pull in the fishing nets. On his final freighter voyage, the massive ship crippled by a typhoon and struggling to keep from sinking, Visko had stared for hours at those twinkling lights, feeling God's presence in the midst of their ocean terror. Stars, unlike people and circumstances and life itself, were constant and predictable, moving across the sky with the seasons, and somehow though planted in the heavens a million miles away those same twinkling stars kept Visko grounded.

He loved his new home and never once had Visko doubted his decision to walk off the *Andrea Doria*, but he missed his homeland. He yearned for the smell of the ocean, the sunlight dancing like sparkling diamonds across the turquoise waters of the Adriatic Sea, the gentle breezes wafting across the waves and ruffling through his hair. And of course he missed his family, his mother and father and his three sisters, and even the baby brother that he'd never had a chance to even know. At night, lying in his bed just before drifting off to sleep, he'd often look up at those familiar stars and somehow it was comforting knowing that far, far away across the Atlantic Ocean, more than 4500 miles from where he was now, his family had said good-night to those same stars before turning into their own beds a few hours earlier.

Cicilija, now seventeen years old, was married. That much he knew, and he couldn't help but grin thinking about his escapade of smuggling that sewing machine from Italy to Stikovica for her marriage dowry. Anita would be fourteen now and Marica ten, growing into pretty young ladies and surely capturing the attention of some silly village boys these days. Baby Ivo wouldn't be much of a baby any more, now four years old and following Ilija up to the farm, learning to be a Njiric man much like he had been taught years ago. Visko wondered about the health of his parents, both of whom were weak and sickly when he left home for the Merchant Marines.

Had it really been just four and a half years ago? So much had happened, so much had changed in that short span of time. But one thing had not and would never change. Visko loved his family and longed to talk with and wondered if he would ever even see them again.

As badly as he wanted to contact his parents and tell them all about his big adventure and new life here in the United States, it was impossible for him to do so. Stikovica had no telephones. Writing a letter to them was out of the question. The Yugoslavian government opened and read every letter that came into their country, and Visko assumed that the American government did the same. If government officials from either or both countries found out about Visko illegally leaving Croatia for America, it would mean imprisonment for his family as well as himself. At least for now, there was no way Visko could safely connect with them, and risk-taker that he was this was one risk he wasn't willing to take.

It wasn't unusual for Ilija and Franica not to hear from Visko for months at a time when he began working on the overseas freighters. Visko reasoned that Ilija would find out from the shipping company about his temporary transfer to the *Andrea Doria*, and as long as there was money for Ilija to pick up at the Dubrovnik office every month they wouldn't be worried. When there was no pay envelope waiting for him, Ilija would surely realize that Visko had quit his job and followed his dream.

Still, Visko couldn't shake the desire to contact his parents when the time was right, but that time wasn't now.

Visko appreciated the sacrifice Nick and his family had made by putting him up in their apartment. Having always enjoyed children, Visko didn't mind watching the toddling son and daughter occasionally, and he was glad to help repay their hospitality by caring for the children while Nick and his wife recovered from a serious auto accident they were involved in while Visko was staying there. Once, when the family dog nipped at Nick's little boy, Visko laughed when the boy turned the tables and bit their pet right on the ear sending the yelping pup to hide from his mischievous perpetrator.

But Visko was chomping at the bit to get a job, a real full-time job, and make his fortune. He had brains and determination, energy and ingenuity. But there was one very important thing he lacked.

"Before you can get a job, Visko, you'll have to have a social security card," Nick told him. Not having any clue what that was, Nick explained that every employer reported his workers' wages to the US government, who took some of every employee's pay for taxes, and that his boss would require him to have a social security number. And in order to file for a social security number, Visko would need an official birth certificate.

"How can I get possibly get a birth certificate?" Visko asked. He didn't even know if his parents had one for him back in Yugoslavia, and he certainly didn't have one himself. So Nick gave him the best advice he knew, and the next morning following Nick's direction, Visko took the train to downtown New York City to find that faithful Croatian Catholic Church at the corner of 8th Avenue and 50th Street. The priest there would surely know what to do.

The aged limestone walls towered above him as he walked through the huge varnished wooden doors. Visko couldn't help but think how much had changed in the few short weeks since he'd first walked past this cathedral his very first day in New York City. How terrified he'd been! Being in the heart of this big city still scared him, but Visko felt much more confident now as he stepped from the bright summer sunlight into the dim quiet of the church. He hadn't been inside more than a few moments when the priest, wearing his traditional cassock, clicked his heels down the marble hallway causing Visko to turn around.

Relief flooded across Visko's face when the priest greeted him in Croatian, and Visko spilled out his story and his request for a birth certificate to the wizened, white-haired man. "Can you help me, please?" Visko pleaded.

Without speaking, the priest faintly nodded his head and the trace of a smile flickered across his face. He turned and beckoned Visko to follow him to an office just down the hallway. Reaching into a drawer of his huge wooden desk, the priest pulled out a tablet and pen.

"I need to ask you a few questions, Visko. When were you born? Who are your parents?" and Visko answered each one, watching as the ink pen in the wrinkled hands of the priest moved across the form filling in the blanks. Knowing Visko had jumped ship and come into America illegally, there was no way to check his credentials, so the priest wrote down each response just as Visko told him.

"Visko Njiric. A nice name, but it doesn't sound very, um, very American. Hmmm..." and he paused in thought for a moment then wrote along a line on the first line of the certificate: Vincent Nerich.

"There you go. The American version of your name. What do you think?"

Visko shrugged his shoulders. Vincent. That was his American name. Vincent. It would take some getting used to, but he liked the way it rolled off his tongue. It sounded so, so... so American! Vincent.

And so, forming his new name silently with his lips as the priest completed the form, carefully tore it off the pad, and stamped the embossed insignia of the Catholic Church at the bottom, Visko left the big church soon afterwards clutching in his hands a church-issued official birth certificate and in his heart his new American identity.

CHAPTER 16

Earning and Learning

July 1956

New York City

English is such a crazy language! Vincent had been in America for over three months now, and as hard as he tried to understand it, the English language just stumped him. The alphabet was similar to the Slavic alphabet, although why the Englishmen who came up with this system felt a need to add letters like Q, X, Y, and W, he had no idea. Croatian was much simpler. Words were spelled like they sounded, with no such craziness as silent letters. Every letter in a word made a sound, and no words had double meanings. Or triple meanings, such as many English words.

Just the simple word "heal". Or "heel" or "he'll." All sounding the exactly the same, but having three totally different spellings and meanings. Words like that are plentiful in English Vincent soon found out, frustrating him over and over again. Sometimes he wondered if he'd ever master this complicated language!

Soon after he'd arrived in New York, Nick had one day taken Vincent to see a family friend who was an English professor at a nearby college. Vincent was eager to learn English and Nick thought perhaps this man could help his cousin learn the language. The professor told Vincent there were two ways to learn English: the proper way, which would take a long time and much studying, or the informal way, a much quicker route. School and studying having never been Vincent's forte combined with the fact that he was in a hurry to learn how to speak in America, Vincent predictably opted for the quick method.

"Go to the movie theater and watch movies. Listen to what is said and match it with the action on the screen, and soon you'll begin to pick up some words and phrases." So that's what Vincent did, paying his way into a movie theater for the 10:00 a.m. showing and sitting through several showings of the same movie until 3:00 the next morning, when the theater shut down for a few hours, and he was forced to leave.

Vincent never forgot his amazement at the first movie he saw, a western film where the cowboy hero died at the end of the show. He couldn't believe his eyes a few minutes later when the movie started over at the beginning and there was that same fellow alive again! Never having seen a motion picture before, Vincent didn't understand how that "miracle" could possibly be so.

The professor also advised Vincent to mingle with his peers, that by hanging out with young men his own age he would learn how to communicate. Of course, that method had its downfall as Vincent learned not only legitimate words but also more than a few words that were best not used in social settings. However, slowly he began to understand more and more and even speak English. He practiced when he could, conversing with others at work, and in the neighborhood, and at home with Nick's family. Even when they laughed at his mispronunciations, misuses of words, and his shaky sentence structure, Vincent may have been temporarily embarrassed but never daunted. He was determined to learn English and become a bona fide United States citizen.

While working on the ships, Vincent had gotten into the habit of occasionally smoking cigarettes with his friends. Marlboro was his favorite brand, but after he arrived in New York City his cigarette-smoking habit caused him much frustration. Try as he might, Vincent couldn't say the word "Marlboro" clearly enough for the gas station or store clerks to understand. So when he couldn't go pick his choice off the shelf on his own, he resorted to asking for "L&M" cigarettes because that was the one brand name he could make them understand. Vincent hated the taste of L&Ms, but his weak English often forced him to settle for them instead.

Over the next several months, Vincent also went to a few night classes taught by a multi-lingual young woman for immigrants like him who were trying to learn English. She was a good teacher and had lots of books in many different languages, but book-learning had never been his thing, and Vincent didn't have a lot of free time once he began working, so he only managed to attend a few of those classes. Gradually, with much listening and practice, English became easier and easier.

Vincent had plenty of opportunities to practice his English skills at his new job, his first full-time position at a machine shop. Uncle Niko had another nephew from his side of the family who was also an illegal immigrant from Yugoslavia, having made his way into New York after jumping ship in Canada. He'd gotten a job at this shop and told his boss about Vincent, getting him a job there too. The owners of the machine shop, two brothers who were themselves immigrants from Malta, especially liked employing illegal young employees since they could work the young men for sometimes eighty hours a week and didn't have to pay them overtime. Vincent, or Vinnie as he quickly became known among his co-workers, was grateful for the job and didn't complain about the hours. At eighty cents an hour, it was the best pay he'd ever had for a full-time job.

Nick had taught Vinnie how to take the bus to the subway station, get on the subway train, get off the subway at the edge of Long Island, then walk five blocks to the machine shop. Vinnie would often take his lunch and even supper sometimes, as many nights he slept on an old couch upstairs above the shop if there wasn't time to go home between shifts. Sometimes Vinnie and his two co-workers would walk to a little diner down on the corner to get a bite to eat. Not speaking English well enough yet, Vinnie would write down his order and give it to the waitress, a kind woman named Pat. He may not have known the English language very well, but Vinnie always understood the language of money, so after paying her, he'd take the bagged food back to the shop for them to eat.

Vinnie had only been working at the machine shop for a few weeks when, the evening of July 26, 1956, as he arrived home exhausted from the day, Uncle Niko was waiting for him with news that took Vinnie's breath away. The *Andrea Doria*, Uncle Niko told him, had crashed and sunk. Uncle Niko knew no more details, so the next morning as he whistled his way down the sidewalk toward the shop, Vinnie slowed as he passed a newspaper vendor cart and the big bold headline proved Uncle Niko's news to be true. He stopped walking, his feet like cement stuck into the sidewalk. A couple of steps backward, and he looked again at the paper, hardly believing his eyes. He couldn't read much English, but he knew what this one said...The *Andrea Doria* had collided with another ship and had sunk to the bottom of the ocean not far off the Nantucket shoreline. Bending closer to see more, the photos of the damaged ship shocked his senses. The collision had happened right in the area of the ship's kitchen! Had Vinnie been aboard that night, he'd have been working his usual night shift baking bread in the kitchen and would surely have been killed.

Arriving back home at Nick's, the whole neighborhood was talking about the biggest news story to rock America in a long while. Vinnie thanked his lucky stars and his God above that he hadn't been on the luxury ocean liner that fateful night. He knew word of the tragedy at sea would soon get back home to his family, and he wondered what they might think, but he wasn't even sure they knew he'd been transferred to the *Andrea Doria*. Contacting them was out of the question now, for fear of getting both them and himself in hot water with their respective governments, but Vinnie felt sure they'd know he was safe when his name didn't show up on the list of casualties.

Vinnie learned so much during those sixteen months that he worked at the machine shop. Not only did he get more proficient with his understanding and speaking English, he also learned a trade and new skills. The shop made dies for hinges, door locks, and other hardware, filling orders as they came. Some weeks were normal, but when a big order needed to be filled, Vinnie and his fellow workers would work double shifts to get it finished. The hours were long, but Vinnie felt it was all worth it when he received his paycheck at the end of each week. By the end of 1956 when Vinnie got his statement for his taxes, he was thrilled to see that he had earned over $4000 since he'd arrived that summer. He felt like a rich man!

It was during his tenure at the machine shop that Vinnie got his driver's license, opening up a whole new world of opportunity for the young man. One day one of the shop's customers offered Vinnie a job working for him as a truck driver, and that he would pay Vinnie $1.60 an hour. That was twice what he was making at the machine shop! He also promised that if Vinnie proved himself to be a good employee, after thirty days, he would up Vinnie's pay to $2.00 per hour. Vinnie told his boss about the offer, saying if they could come close to the $1.60 he'd rather stay at the machine shop. His boss's argument that the machine shop was a much better opportunity, that anyone could be a truck driver but that Vinnie was learning a marketable skill and might someday become a machinist himself fell on deaf ears. At that time for Vinnie, more money now spoke much louder than future possibilities. It was just too good to pass up, so Vinnie thanked the machine shop owners and went to work as a delivery truck driver in downtown New York City.

The trucking company was owned by five Jewish brothers. The main office, run by the oldest brother, was on 26th Street in downtown Manhattan with the factory where Vinnie reported for work being located in Brooklyn. The factory was four floors high with each of the other four brothers in charge of their own floor. Vinnie was often confused working for them, as the brothers did not seem to cooperate with each other very well, and oftentimes Vinnie was torn about which brother's orders he should follow. So he did his best to keep his head down and his mouth shut and get in and out of the factory with the orders as quickly as he could.

By this time, Vinnie had moved out of Nick's home into his own apartment. Nick had been a great help to Vinnie in his first year in America, but Vinnie had saved enough money and felt enough confidence to move out on his own. When the weather was nice, Vinnie would ride his bicycle from his new basement studio apartment in Long Island to the factory, a 45-minute commute that included riding across the pedestrian walkway alongside the Queens Bridge. On the days he had to use public transportation instead, the commute was about 30 minutes longer as he had to take the train into Grand Central Station, transfer onto the Coney Island train, and then transfer again to get where he was going. Getting around New York City was a maze in itself, and Vinnie much preferred the ride on his dependable bicycle to maneuvering through the craziness of train stations. Either way, he soon discovered, the best way to beat the crowds was to get up and out very early in the morning, as he'd rather wait for the factory to open than to be stuck in the madness that was New York City rush hour.

Metal shelving for offices, steel door frames, metal factory chairs, and steel partitions were among Vinnie's most common loads for delivery. Driving a car was one thing, but maneuvering a two-ton sixteen-foot box truck through the heart of Manhattan was not for the faint-hearted. As soon as the warehouse opened, Vinnie, having already loaded his first delivery onto the truck the evening before, was ready to go. His bosses were pleased with their new eager employee, as Vinnie worked twice as hard as the fellow he'd replaced. Instead of making just one delivery per day, Vinnie was able to make two. Timing his afternoon departure from the factory for 1:00 p.m.

when the traffic was lightest, Vinnie was able to double what the other delivery driver had done. And then, after his day's deliveries were finished, Vinnie stopped at the downtown office every day to drop off the paperwork.

Although Vinnie had clearly proved himself to be a good employee, and despite reminding his boss of the promise to raise his pay to $2.00 per hour after the first thirty days and even threatening to quit, Vinnie never got the promised raise. But he was smart enough to know better than to quit a job before finding another one, so after working as a delivery driver for about six months Vinnie decided it was time to keep his eyes and ears open for another job opportunity to present itself.

Vinnie had one more goal to reach before he could finally relax into his new American life. More than anything in the world, he wanted to be a US citizen.

CHAPTER 17

Heartbreak in Stikovica

End of July 1956

Stikovica, Yugoslavia

Franica knew something was terribly, horribly wrong before Ilija even opened his mouth to speak. Anguish was written all over his face...in his tragic eyes, his pale countenance, his quivering mouth. She steadied herself against the table, afraid of what she didn't yet know.

Ilija took a deep breath, pulling out a chair at the table and gesturing for his wife to sit down. She followed his hand, lowering herself onto the wooden seat without ever taking her eyes off his face. Ilija sat down beside her, clenching his fists together on the tabletop.

When he finally opened his mouth, dreading himself to hear his own words, he didn't mince them. "The *Andrea Doria* collided with a Swedish ship last night, just a few miles off the American coast. Many people were killed in the accident. The ship sunk this morning, and there is no word yet on survivors."

Franica felt her heart fall into her stomach and the kitchen began to spin. What was Ilija saying? She knew very well what he was telling her, but her mind refused to listen. Visko, their eldest son, was the baker on board the *Andrea Doria*.

"Oh Ilija! What about our Visko?!" she cried out, bringing her hands to her face in shock and disbelief. "Visko, my dear boy Visko!" And try as she might to hold them back, the tears began rolling down her tan cheeks.

Ilija tried his best to comfort her, reaching deep down inside himself hoping he had enough strength for them both. "Visko is a strong boy, Franica. He is fine. I know he is okay. He is a strong swimmer and a good thinker. If anyone can survive a shipwreck, it is our Visko." Trying to convince his wife, he began to feel a little better about the situation himself. Yes, if anyone was a survivor it was his son Visko, Ilija thought proudly.

Taking Franica by the shoulders, he looked into her teary eyes. "I heard about the accident in the village this morning; everyone was talking about it. No one can believe that the *Andrea Doria*, of all ships, is gone. But our Visko is okay. I am sure of it!" And he hastily kissed her tear-stained cheek and hurried out the door and down the rocky seashore to his boat. Ilija would go to the shipping office in Dubrovnik. The agency officials would know what happened, and they would assure him that Visko is alive and well.

The last time Ilija had gone to pick up Visko's pay envelope, as he did each month, the agency officer had told him about Visko's temporary transfer to the *Andrea Doria*. With his assigned freighter in dry dock for 30-60 days for repair, Ilija was told, Visko had agreed to serve as a temporary worker for the Italian cruise ship. Discovering that Visko's new monthly wages were $30 instead of the $14 he was making before, Ilija smiled with pride at his son. What a wise decision Visko had made! That boy, as aggravating as he could be at times, has a good, albeit stubborn, head on his shoulders.

And that same good stubborn head would serve him well in a shipwreck, just as it had served him well during wartime. Ilija was feeling ever more hopeful as he tied up his boat at the dock and walked as fast as his tired legs could carry him to the office of Visko's shipping company.

Everywhere he went, along every street, he overheard folks talking about the tragedy. The *Andrea Doria*, the seemingly unsinkable *Andrea Doria* laying now at the bottom of the Atlantic? No one could believe that could possibly be true. And yet it was, the agency assured Ilija, although they had no news to give him about his son. Come back in a few days, they told Ilija.

And so he did. Every few days, Ilija made the trip to Dubrovnik, hoping this time to find out the whereabouts of his son. As photographs of the sea disaster made their way onto front pages of the village newspapers, it was clear to see that where the *Andrea Doria* had been struck was right in the area of the ship's kitchen. Seeing those photographs alarmed Ilija, but he didn't dare show them to Franica. Surely, even though the wreckage may have looked very bad, somehow Visko had survived and Ilija tried not to dwell on the haunting photos of the grand ship just before it collapsed to its watery grave.

One day, seeing Ilija coming in the door, the man in charge at the shipping office beckoned Ilija to the window. Ilija's heart smiled as he saw the gentleman holding in his hand what must be the *Andrea Doria's* manifest, but as they scanned the list of names together his smile quickly dimmed and his hopes crumbled. Visko's name was not listed at all. The officer explained that since Visko was temporary help and not actually employed by the Italian ship line, he wouldn't have even been listed on the manifest at all.

No news is good news, Ilija told himself and tried to convince Franica. Their Visko was surely alive and would contact them soon. But when weeks passed with no letter and no word about his whereabouts, Ilija and Franica and Grandma Njiric and the entire family began to face what they dreaded but deep down knew must be true.

Visko was lost at sea and presumed dead.

Finally, with heavy hearts, the Njirics resigned themselves that it was time to stop hoping and face reality. Ilija decided that the period of wishful thinking was over, and the family must quit putting their lives on hold and deal with the awful truth. Franica and Grandma donned their black mourning dresses, dresses they would wear for the next twelve months. Tears from Franica's face dropped onto Ilija's shirt in her hands as she sewed the traditional black patch across his sleeve. The family's year-long mourning period had begun for their eldest son, the Njiric family heir lost at sea, their eighteen-year-old Visko.

Since there was no body to bury, an empty wooden coffin was brought to the Njiric home. As word got out that the family was ready to proceed with a funeral, neighbors and relatives poured into the home bearing baskets of food and their condolences to the family. Everyone knew Visko, and they shared stories about his escapades and reminisced about his all-too-short life. Following the traditions of generations of Croatians before them, the next morning the wreath-laden coffin was lifted onto the shoulders of several of Visko's cousins and childhood friends, leading a walking funeral procession up the rocky mountain path about a mile or so to the village cemetery and its chapel, the sad songs of the mourning troupe drifting down to the sea. After a full funeral mass in the chapel, the family gathered in the cemetery outside. Franica wiped away tears as the marble slab covering the family grave was pulled aside, and Visko's coffin was laid to rest alongside his Njiric forefathers.

This was the saddest day of Franica's life, and she was exhausted. After several long draining weeks of waiting and hoping, she had just laid her firstborn to rest. How ironic it was, she thought, that the sea which Visko had loved since his first breath upon its aqua waves was where he also had taken his last. He was a good Catholic boy, and she knew in her heart that Visko would spend eternity with God, and one day she would see him again. But she wasn't yet ready to let him go.

In the back of her mind, the thought nagged at her. Perhaps he wasn't really dead at all. Everything in her told her the opposite; the fact that he'd not contacted them should be proof enough. Yet as slim as it was, although she dare not breathe it to Ilija, she just couldn't give up wondering and hoping in her heart of hearts that it really wasn't so.

Keeping Visko alive in her mind was the only way Franica could keep her heart from breaking completely in two.

photo by Zachary Nirich

Visko's grave, his empty coffin buried with his grandfather Visko Njiric
and later his father Ilija "Puho" Njiric

CHAPTER 18

Letters

Summer 1957

Back and forth, across the Atlantic Ocean

Vinnie licked the stamp and stuck it on the front of the envelope, just above and to the right of the mailing address: Ilija Njiric, 29 Stikovica, Dubrovnik, Yugoslavia. For months and months now, ever since he had found out about the sinking of the *Andrea Doria* last July, he'd desperately wanted to write a letter to his parents back in Yugoslavia. Vinnie knew Ilija and Franica and Grandma, indeed the whole Njiric clan, must be worried sick about him.

But it was for their own good that he hadn't yet written. And for his too. Knowing that all letters coming into and going out of Yugoslavia were opened and screened by government officials, Vinnie feared his family might get in trouble since their son had illegally left the country. But, if he were honest with himself, even more than that he feared for his own future. If the US government should open his letters and find out he was in America illegally, they would surely find him and deport him back to Yugoslavia. After dreaming so long and working so hard to get to America, Vinnie wasn't about to let a little letter betray him and derail his future, so for nearly a year, he resisted the urge to write.

Over the past year, he'd come a long way and learned a lot. And one of the things he'd learned was that, unlike his home country, the US officials did not open personal mail. Apparently, they didn't care about the mundane details of personal communication like his own Communist country. So, after mulling it over for a couple of weeks, Vinnie decided to take the risk.

The letter was short and to the point. Addressing it to his mother and father, Vinnie told them he was in America, that he'd jumped ship in New York City before the *Andrea Doria's* sinking, and that he was alive and doing well. Still reluctant to give too many details, he folded the paper, stuck it in the envelope, and smiled as he dropped it in the mail slot.

One month later

Stikovica, Yugoslavia

Ilija stared at the envelope for a few moments before opening it. "New York, New York," the return address read. Perhaps another letter from his sister Maria? But no, the handwriting was different, somehow vaguely familiar. His curiosity piqued as he read and re-read the words.

The letter was from Visko. Or someone claiming to be Visko. How could that be? Visko had perished in the *Andrea Doria* tragedy nearly a year ago. His memory was buried in the family grave, the dreadful period of mourning was nearly over, and the family was ready to move on with their lives. What kind of cruel joke was this?

Few details were offered by the writer of the letter. Simply that he was their son Visko, alive and well in New York City. So many unanswered questions... could he really be their son?!

As Ilija read the letter to his wife and mother, Franica's heart jumped for joy. Could it really be true, that her Visko was living and breathing in America? She hardly dared herself the thought, but all these months her mother's intuition had not quite laid her hopes to rest. And now, perhaps her fervent prayers had been answered.

Franica sat at the table as Ilija penned his reply:

"If you are my son, answer these three questions. No one outside of our family would know the answers: What was the biggest fish you and I ever caught? What kind of bait did we use to catch it? How did you get the scar on your left foot?"

Three weeks later

Flushing, New York

So they'd received the letter! Such easy questions to answer, and Vinnie grinned as he put his own pen to paper.

"The biggest fish we ever caught together was a 22-kilo sea bass. We had baited a line from the shore with a baby octopus, fishing for moray eel but caught the huge sea bass instead.

And the scar on my foot? That was when the piece of wood you threw at my head missed and hit my foot instead."

How well Vinnie remembered that incident from his childhood. Ilija had gotten a brand new wooden fishing boat, and the floor of the boat was made with wooden slats providing a level dry footing and allowing any water that got inside the boat to drain down underneath. Ilija was proud of his new boat and cautioned his children never to jump into the boat lest one of the slats break.

Carelessly ignoring his father's admonition, one afternoon Visko had taken a flying leap from the pier into the boat and heard a loud "snap." Sure enough, one of the slats had broken under the impact. Knowing he'd be in big trouble if Ilija found out, he tried to hide the broken slat by covering it with the coil of anchor rope and hoped Ilija wouldn't notice. Or at the very least, that when he did, Ilija would think he'd somehow broken it himself.

Smiling at the memory, just as Visko had feared Ilija had been livid when he discovered the broken slat. Demanding who had broken it, Visko had yelled, "I don't know" from the beach.

But Ilija wasn't fooled. "Don't lie to me!" and in his anger Ilija had picked up the splintered board and flung it toward Visko's head. Visko leaped aside to avoid the board and instead the splintered slat impaled itself into his foot, permanently leaving a scar.

Mailing his letter with the answers to Ilija's questions, Vinnie felt a huge weight lifted, a weight he hadn't even realized was there. In his determination to make his way in his new country, Vinnie had never really left his family behind in his old country, nor would he ever. One month from now, Ilija would receive this reply and Vinnie could picture him opening the letter and excitedly reading it aloud to his mother and grandmother. Vinnie knew how surprised and relieved they would be to know that he was alive and doing well in the United States, and that one day they would indeed see him again.

A family restored, broken hearts healed... the power of just a few letters.

CHAPTER 19

More Earning and Learning

Spring 1958

New York City

Four thousand dollars. FOUR THOUSAND DOLLARS!!! It might as well have been one million in Vinnie's mind. When Vinnie had gone to a lawyer Nick knew soon after arriving in America to tell him that he wanted to become a legal American citizen, the lawyer's instructions had been this: "Keep your mouth shut, work hard, and come back to see me when you've saved up $4000."

That number danced constantly in Vinnie's head, and it kept him focused during the 80-hour work weeks at the machine shop, and as he drove the delivery truck through the traffic-jammed streets of Manhattan. Whatever it took, as quickly as possible, he had to save $4000.

So Vinnie worked hard, always looking for new opportunities for full-time, good-paying work as well as picking up part-time jobs on the weekends. Sometimes it seemed he was working all the time, but Vinnie had a goal in front of him, and nothing was going to get in his way.

After six months of working for five bickering brothers driving a delivery truck through downtown New York City, Vinnie found out about a position with the Painters and Decorators Union and was quickly hired. Vinnie would report to the Union Hall for his painting assignments, which took him to all sorts of jobs all over the New York City area. Sometimes the jobs were fairly simple like painting new or remodeled units in an apartment complex. Other jobs were high-risk and complicated; on one particularly dangerous job, Vinnie was responsible to refill buckets of paint for other painters on a skyscraper under construction, carrying a five-gallon paint bucket in each hand as he walked the steel beams in the open air 30 stories above the street with no safety devices at all. One false step and he would have been a goner. Being small, sure-footed, and fearless worked to Vinnie's advantage on jobs like those, and he never suffered a mishap or serious injury.

Once the union sent him to the huge Johnson & Johnson factory in New Jersey to replace all of the thousands of light bulbs on the entire campus, a much easier job that took him two weeks to complete. Sometimes he would assist an electrician doing repairs in a clothing factory, working in a vast room full of women sitting in front of humming sewing machines. Vinnie had never seen so many sewing machines in one room, and he recalled the time he smuggled the Italian sewing machine to his father. Had that really been only a couple of years ago? It seemed like a couple of lifetimes.

Vinnie was sometimes amazed at the colors people chose for their apartments, and still not always reliably understanding what people said, he questioned the union foreman who told him to paint one lady's kitchen black. Black? Was he understanding correctly? So he had the foreman write it down, and when he went to pick up the can of paint that day, he used the can with "B-L-A-C-K" written on the top. Yes black, a black kitchen. Not quite as bad as the black kitchen, but Vinnie shook his head another time as he rolled dark bold purple paint onto the brand new walls of one apartment's bedroom. Sometimes American people could be so very strange!

Window-washing was a part-time job that Vinnie did for a while, once again working several stories up on the outsides of tall apartment buildings. At least he did have a harness support for this perilous job; Vinnie would open the windows then sit on the outside ledges and, bringing the window down into his lap, he would squeegee the glass squeaky clean. Once again his nerves of steel and nimble body served him well, as Vinnie scrambled from window to window, earning fifteen cents for each sparkling clean one. Vinnie also helped with gardening work for a landscape company, pulling weeds and planting flowers, whatever needed to be done. Another part-time job, Vinnie worked alongside a man who had a business sealing basements. He'd dig around the foundation and help put tar and tar paper around the outside to stop it from leaking, then fill the dirt back in around it.

New York City winters provided other chances for Vinnie to make money. When the huge snowfalls came, the Department of Sanitation needed extra truck drivers to pick up the snow loads and dump them into the harbor. Vinnie was grateful for the work, even if it did mean scraping the snow off the seat of his window-less 1947 Studebaker and slip-sliding his way through the New York City streets to the Sanitation Department's office to get the truck. One blustery morning, Vinnie was stopped by a police car on his way to do just that. During snow emergencies, only authorized vehicles were allowed on the streets, and his beat-up car certainly wasn't authorized. Thankfully, Vinnie had put on that morning the Sanitation Department-issued official shirt, or he'd surely have gotten himself a ticket. Instead, the police officers left him with some good advice which he took the following spring when he traded in his junky-although-beloved old Studebaker for something a lot more respectable and reliable.

Saturdays Vinnie always seemed to find a way to earn a few extra bucks. But, he tried his best not to work on Sundays. Just as he had learned as a child back in Yugoslavia, Sunday was God's day, and he faithfully attended a Catholic Church near where he was living at the time nearly every Sunday. Twice a year he dutifully went to confession as prescribed by his church, and lived his faith as his mother and grandmother had taught him as best he could being a young, single man living in New York City.

Vinnie really had very little free time, which was probably a good thing as a lonely young man in a big city could get himself into girl trouble pretty quickly. He had a couple of casual girlfriends during those first years in New York. On one of his movie theater English-learning sessions, he met a nice girl and they saw each other a few times, but since she lived quite a distance away from Vinnie's apartment, that relationship was short-lived. Another girlfriend happened to live conveniently just a couple of buildings down, the daughter of his landlord. She was a very sweet patient girl, and Vinnie enjoyed the brief opportunities they spent together. While some people didn't want to spend a lot of time and energy on someone who couldn't speak English, she was nice and patient and in fact helped Vinnie a great deal with his English skills.

But Vinnie wasn't ready to get serious with any girl. Not only did he not have much time, he also wasn't willing to spend his hard-earned money on dating. Every extra dollar he earned he was saving to pay the lawyer to get his citizenship papers, and until that goal was reached Vinnie didn't have eyes or energy for much else.

Every job Vinnie took, he learned new skills and made new connections. And he always had his eyes and ears open for a new, better opportunity. So, when an acquaintance told him that the neighborhood junior high school was looking for a janitor, Vinnie went in to apply for the custodial position with the New York City Board of Education. His English was still not fluent, although he could understand the language much better than he could speak it. However, that didn't matter as he'd be working from 3:00 in the afternoon until midnight, after the students were gone home and the school was empty.

Quiet and calm, the after-hours school custodial job was about as far from the harrowing downtown delivery and the risky painting jobs as Vinnie could imagine. Vinnie was hired as the school's head custodian or, as he laughingly called himself, "The Head Sweeper" as that was mostly what he did every evening. He swept stairways and hallways and classrooms, emptied trashcans and used pitchforks to throw all the trash to be burned into the furnace in the school's basement. If there were after-school activities, Vinnie would have extra work cleaning up the gymnasium or auditorium. It was a good job, steady work, and it was during this time that Vinnie met his first real love.

CHAPTER 20

Love and Legalities

1959

New York City

Margaret strolled into Vinnie's life one day as Vinnie and his friend Norman were walking out of a movie theater. Flipping her dark curly hair and giggling with her girlfriend, the two teenagers were leaving the same movie as Vinnie and Norman. The young men didn't know the girls but Norman, always ready for an excuse to drive his car, sidled up beside them and asked if they wanted to go for a ride. Surprisingly, the girls agreed, and the four of them hopped into Norman's car for a spin through the city.

Vinnie immediately hit it off with Margaret. Perhaps not jaw-dropping gorgeous, but she was pretty enough and, more importantly to Vinnie, she seemed kind and sweet. Giggling as he spoke, she was charmed by his accent and shaky English. She lived within walking distance of Vinnie, and the two quickly became friends.

He didn't have much time or money to spend on a serious relationship, but Vinnie had to admit it was nice to have a girlfriend, someone to hang out with and with whom to share his dreams. Margaret was patient and kind, and the two began double-dating with Norman and Margaret's friend whenever they got the chance.

After a few fun dates with the four of them together, Margaret invited Vinnie to dinner at her home, so her parents could meet her new young man.

Margaret was of Scotch-Irish descent, and she and her older brother lived with their parents in a middle-class neighborhood several blocks from Vinnie's Long Island apartment. Her mother was a devout Catholic and the children were raised Catholic, even though her father had nothing much to do with the church. Margaret's father, a jovial friendly guy, shook Vinnie's hand heartily and liked him immediately. Margaret's mother, a short spunky Scottish woman, proved, however, to be a little more difficult to figure out.

Despite an awkward first dinner meeting, Margaret's parents apparently approved of her young beau, and Vinnie and Margaret began dating. Margaret's father would often pick Vinnie up in his car after he got off work and take him to an Irish bar for a beer with a shot of whiskey. He clearly liked Vinnie and approved of the relationship, especially since he was getting a new drinking buddy. Vinnie spent a lot of time just hanging out with them at her parents' house as the car he was driving at the time, that old 1947 Studebaker with no windows, was certainly not fit for squiring a date around. Besides that, Vinnie didn't have extra money he was willing to spend on restaurants and movies with a girl, so most of their dates consisted of walking down the block to a book shop or stopping for an ice cream cone or soda at the drugstore. She was a friend, someone fun with whom to spend his free time, and for Vinnie that was more than enough.

Never one to turn down an opportunity to earn a few extra dollars, Vinnie was doing part-time odd jobs when he got the chance, as well as working full-time as a janitor at the nearby middle school, saving every dollar he could toward his $4000 goal. The only real splurge Vinnie had allowed himself was a car, realizing that he needed reliable transportation and a vehicle in which Margaret could ride without being embarrassed. Vinnie had traded in his beat-up, window-less 1947 Studebaker for a shiny new 1958 red-and-white Chevrolet convertible. Driving through the streets of New York with Margaret at his side in his brand-spanking-new ride, Vinnie felt like he had finally achieved his dream. Almost. He hadn't quite become a citizen yet, but he was well on his way.

Putting away every dollar he could spare, Vinnie was inching ever closer to his $4000 goal. Watching his bank account grow slowly but steadily, Vinnie could hardly wait! When Tete Eva, his rich aunt from California who had solidified his dream of coming to America when she had visited the Njirics in 1950, found out about his goal, she had sent Vinnie $1000 to help out. Working and saving, the once seemingly impossible amount of money was finally looking attainable. He was almost there!

Seeming like a lifetime ago, and indeed it was in many ways, Vinnie couldn't contain his excitement as he drove his new car to see his lawyer in the summer of 1959, the required $4000 in hand. This was it, the day he'd worked for the past three years! But unfortunately, like all things governmental, becoming a citizen wasn't going to be quite as easy as Vinnie thought.

After Vinnie handed him the money, the lawyer instructed him, "Don't go anywhere. Two men will come to get you. There's nothing to worry about. They will take care of you." Vinnie wasn't quite sure what that meant, but if it was a necessary step toward citizenship, he would do whatever was required.

The next day, a Friday afternoon, just as the lawyer had promised, Vinnie saw them coming and watched from his basement apartment window as two official-looking men dressed in black suits with dark sunglasses walked down the stairs and knocked on the door. Showing Vinnie their identification, the men were detectives from the US Immigration Department and asked for Vincent Nerich. "That's me," Vinnie answered them.

"May we please see your green card?" one man very seriously

inquired.

Vinnie felt his heart beating a little faster as he shook his head and quietly replied, "I don't have one."

"You'll need to come with us," and the two men escorted Vinnie out the door and up the stairs toward their black parked car.

With Vinnie in the back of the car, wondering where the detectives were taking him, they drove onto a ferry that was crossing over the harbor to a place that had awed Vinnie ever since he had arrived in New York City over three years before. Parking the car, the detective opened the back door, and Vinnie stepped out at the base of the Statue of Liberty. They were on Ellis Island.

Leading Vinnie inside the building that forms the base of the country's most iconic statue, the officers pointed down a tiled hallway, and Vinnie followed them to a large office where a man motioned for him to sit across the desk from him. As the man questioned Vinnie, a very nice Croatian man was there translating for him, helping Vinnie and the immigration officer understand each other. The officer filled out the paperwork as Vinnie responded to his queries. Thinking he'd at last be getting his citizenship papers in his hand very soon, Vinnie wasn't worried at all but was in fact excited. It was really happening!

But after the paperwork was finished, the man didn't hand him anything at all. Instead, the two detectives loaded him back into the car and took Vinnie downtown to the immigration detention center on 10th Street in downtown Manhattan, a weathered 25-story building with bars and grids of wire on the windows. Onto the elevator and up to the tenth floor, the two detectives led him off and through a set of double swinging doors that led into three huge rooms lined with stacks of beds. A jail of sorts, guarded by an old unarmed man in uniform standing by the door, Vinnie walked into one of the rooms where he joined several other illegal immigrants who were already there. Vinnie guessed there must be about one hundred people between those three rooms. Walking inside as the detectives spoke quietly with the guard, Vinnie looked down from the window onto the street. Just below the window was a church along with people walking back and forth on the sidewalk. Being late Friday afternoon, it was Vinnie's misfortune that since no government offices were open on Saturday or Sunday, he ended up spending two days and two nights in the detention center. As he watched from the barred window, Vinnie longed to be one of those New Yorkers, looking, from ten stories up, like tiny dolls dressed in their hats and fancy clothing, filing into that church on Sunday morning. Instead, he felt like a trapped animal, counting the minutes as they ever-so-slowly passed with hopes that on Monday morning Vinnie would get out of this place.

Late Monday morning, an officer talked with the guard and walked over to Vinnie and told him he was free on bond. His lawyer was waiting for him downstairs, having posted the required $1000 bond to bail Vinnie out. Assuring him that he was working to get a court date for his citizenship hearing, Vinnie went back to work and waited for word from the lawyer. Nothing was simple, it seemed, and as anxious as Vinnie was to get this finalized, the government and its complicated political machinery was in no hurry at all. Days and weeks passed with no word, and Vinnie's frustration grew as time marched relentlessly onward.

By late summer 1959, it was painfully apparent to Vinnie that Margaret (as well as her mother) was ready for their relationship to get much more serious. Yes, Vinnie supposed he loved her. But he certainly wasn't convinced that Margaret was the love of his life and didn't feel ready to settle down quite yet. However, eventually, after dating for nearly a year, Vinnie caved to Margaret's pressure and her mother was delighted when the two of them, after consulting with the priest, announced they were going to get married.

And so they did in the fall of 1959, Vinnie wearing a black tux with white ruffled shirt and Margaret looking lovely in her traditional wedding gown, tying the knot during a traditional wedding mass at the altar of the Catholic Church where Margaret's family attended, witnessed by a group of family and friends. Margaret's parents hosted a reception at their home following the ceremony, and before he even realized it and much sooner than he had planned, Vinnie had a wife, and the couple set up housekeeping in a small Long Island apartment.

One of the neighbors who lived in the same apartment house where Vinnie and Margaret had made their home came up to Vinnie as he was getting out of his car one evening. Vinnie knew who he was, a friendly man who went to their church, and the two often waved when they passed each other. As the neighbor began talking to Vinnie, he asked if Vinnie might like to join the Knights of Columbus where he was already a member. Vinnie was flattered at the friendly invitation, and even though he really didn't know much at all about the Catholic men's organization at that time, he agreed to go with his neighbor to the next meeting as a guest; a few meetings later, Vinnie found himself the newest member of the Knights of Columbus. Feeling that he was finally being accepted into American society, Vinnie was so proud to be asked to carry the US flag for the K of C in a big city parade.

Through their membership together, Vinnie and his neighbor eventually became good friends. His friend, Vinnie learned, was a captain in the FBI, in charge of the FBI headquarters in downtown New York. A few months later he approached Vinnie with a job opportunity as a janitor in the FBI building and encouraged Vinnie to apply for the good-paying job, so that's what Vinnie did.

Vinnie didn't get the job. The FBI building was heated by a massive water boiler furnace system, the likes of with which Vinnie had no experience or knowledge. That being a critical part of the position, Vinnie's employment application was turned down. Vinnie was a little disappointed, but he was doing fine with his job at the school and life was good, so he soon forgot about the whole incident.

Finally, after months and months of waiting, Vinnie got the phone call from his lawyer. The court date was set for his immigration hearing!

Entering the court room with his lawyer at his side, Vinnie couldn't contain the butterflies in his stomach. At the front of the huge elegant room sat the judge in his black robe, and he beckoned toward Vinnie and his lawyer to come forward and stand in front of his bench.

Looking Vinnie straight in the eye, the judge asked him, "Vincent Nerich, do you want to stay in this country?"

"Yes, sir," Vinnie answered.

"We don't need any trouble-makers; we've already got plenty of those," the judge countered.

"No, sir. I'm not a trouble-maker, sir. I've never been in any trouble," Vinnie replied.

"Well then, I hope that is true, and that you've never been in any trouble or caused any problem with someone. Before we can issue you citizenship papers, we need to investigate and be sure you are telling me the truth."

Vinnie had no problem with that. He had nothing to hide. Since there was no US Embassy in Communist Yugoslavia, the judge explained that the court would have to send two government agents, one from the FBI and one from the Immigration Department over to Dubrovnik to check out Vinnie's story.

"Okay," Vinnie thought, and nodded at the judge.

"You will be responsible to pay those expenses," the judge told Vinnie, and his lawyer agreed that they would pay the cost for two officials to make the trip. Vinnie wrote a letter to his family telling them to expect the visitors. As it turned out, the officers arrived in Stikovica before Vinnie's letter, catching the villagers and

Vinnie's family by surprise and creating quite a stir in the village.

A couple of months later, Vinnie and his lawyer were called back to see the judge again, this time in his chamber. The government agents, who had cost Vinnie a staggering additional $1000 each for their expenses, had returned with their report. Traveling to Stikovica, they'd asked the Njiric family and neighbors about Vinnie, if he'd ever been in trouble, if he was a member of the Communist Party, if he'd ever killed anybody, lots of questions about Vinnie's past trustworthiness and character.

Inside the judge's chamber, joined by the FBI and Immigration agents, as well as his lawyer, Vinnie's eyes got big and he gulped when the judge sternly said, "Our report shows there is a problem. You did indeed get into trouble before you left Yugoslavia."

Vinnie couldn't imagine to what the judge could possibly be referring. Of course, he'd been a little mischievous as a boy, but he'd never really done anything wrong, never had any dealings with the law. What was the judge talking about?

"It seems," the judge went on, his eyes beady as he stared at Vinnie over the top of his wire-rimmed glasses, "that perhaps you were lying. You told me you had not been in any trouble and had not committed any crime."

"No sir, Your Honor," Vinnie managed to get out over the lump that was quickly forming in his throat.

"A lady [which he named] from your village has a different story to tell. She claims you stole seven apples from her tree one time."

Vinnie wanted to burst out laughing, but it was clear that the judge didn't think it was funny. Looking so serious, the judge asked Vinnie, "Is that true?"

Not quite knowing how he should answer, Vinnie shrugged his shoulders. Really??? Surely a few picked apples from his childhood would not stand in the way of his dream! The judge stared down at the paperwork in front of him, shuffling the pages back and forth for a few very long moments before looking back up at Vinnie over his glasses.

The judge spoke. "Okay, Vincent can stay here," and Vinnie finally allowed himself to breathe again. "But, since you did it illegally the first time, you will have to leave the country and re-enter legally, get a green card, and then eventually you can become a citizen."

The lawyer agreed to work out the details. He wrote a letter to the government officials in Canada, asking them to help. Canada denied, citing too much paperwork and bother as the reason. So he wrote the same letter to Mexico, stating Vinnie's dilemma, and the government of Mexico likewise turned them down. Frustrated, the lawyer called Vinnie. "You may have to go back to Europe and then come back here."

"I don't want to go back to Europe!" Vinnie exclaimed, thinking of all he had gone through to finally get into America. "There has to be another way. Where else can I go?"

Thinking for a moment, his lawyer had another idea. "What about the Bahamas? You could go to the Bahamas and then re-enter the United States. But it might cost you a little money."

There was no turning back now. "Sure, let's try it," Vinnie answered. At this point, he was willing to do just about anything to get this legal headache behind him.

When the phone rang a couple of days later, the lawyer had good news. The Bahamas government would accept Vinnie and help them out, with certain conditions. During Vinnie's stay, he would have to spend one thousand US dollars and stay at least forty-eight hours in that island country.

Another $1000? How quickly the original $4000 had turned

into $7000! (Thankfully, with his aunt's gracious donation and his lawyer giving him a little bit of a break, Vinnie "only" had to come up with $5000 on his own, still a hefty chunk of money for the young man.) But, what choice did he have? So Vinnie agreed and, wanting to help his cousin out, Nick bought Vinnie a $200 round-trip ticket to the Bahamas. Nick took Vinnie to the New York City airport to catch his flight, bearing an official letter from the Immigration Department in lieu of a passport, and for the first time in his twenty-two years Vinnie flew on an airplane.

After scrimping money for so long, Vinnie found the task of spending $1000 in just two short days very, very difficult. He hated spending his hard-earned money, and he wasn't a shopper. Vinnie got himself a room in an expensive hotel, ordering food service and leaving big tips, always asking for a receipt to prove he'd followed the agreement.

Vinnie bought ten postcards, giving the vendor with an extra $20 tip. Vinnie paid a taxi to drive him on a tour of the island, exchanging a very generous tip for a piece of paper that would act as a receipt. Not forgetting his wife back home, Margaret would receive a couple of small souvenirs that added to Vinnie's total. Playing the Big Spender was a difficult role for the penny-pinching young fellow, especially in those days when prices were low and items were inexpensive. With just a few hours left and still a wad of bills yet to spend, Vinnie went into a casino and gambled it away, first asking the casino owner to be sure he could get a written receipt, entering into a silent agreement that benefited them both when the owner put down a larger amount than Vinnie had actually spent and Vinnie gave him a $50 tip for doing so. Spending money was exhausting. However, before he left the Bahamas Vinnie did keep his end of the bargain, and he re-entered the US at the New York City airport, showed his letter and the required spending receipts, and was issued a legal green card by the immigration officials there.

A GREEN CARD!!! After all those legal shenanigans and

spending more money than he'd planned, in August of 1960, after four years of being an illegal immigrant, Vinnie had finally earned legal status in the United States of America. In just three more years, Vinnie was told, he'd be able to apply and test for citizenship. Finally, his dream was on its way to coming true!

Celebration time! Nick, so happy for his cousin, treated Vinnie and Margaret, his lawyer and the lawyer's secretary, and other friends and family to dinner and drinks at a nice restaurant to celebrate Vinnie's green card. Vinnie had never been happier!

Floating on air for a couple of weeks, Vinnie's heart quickly sunk and his feet came back down to earth when he received in the mail a letter from the FBI. Opening and reading the letter, Vinnie discovered that officials at the FBI wanted to see him.

Wondering why he was being summoned, Vinnie went downtown and walked into the FBI Headquarters in New York City, carrying the letter in his hands. He was familiar with the building, having gone there to apply for the janitorial position a while back. Vinnie walked up to the reception desk and handed his letter to the man behind it. After reading the letter, the man looked back up at Vinnie and demanded that he immediately go down the hall and report to the first office on the right. Why so mean, Vinnie wondered? He'd done nothing wrong, nothing at all.

Knocking on the closed wooden door shiny with aged varnish, Vinnie was puzzled. He had no idea why he was here and why everyone seemed so angry. Behind the door, a deep voice spoke. "Come in." Reading the letter Vinnie handed to him, the man looked up at Vinnie and demanded sternly, "Why haven't you reported for the draft?"

"What?" Vinnie thought. "What are you talking about?" he answered aloud.

"Don't get smart with me, young man. You know what I'm talking about."

Vinnie shook his head. "No. No, I don't," Vinnie answered truthfully. Vinnie didn't know that he was supposed to report for the draft. The man was irate. Confused and frustrated, Vinnie met the man's harsh stare and timidly asked if his neighbor/friend still worked there for the FBI.

"How do you know my captain?" the man demanded.

"He's my friend and neighbor, and we go to the same church."

At that, the man picked up his phone and soon the Captain walked into the office. "Hey! What are you doing over here?" greeting Vinnie with a smile and handshake.

The other FBI man answered for Vinnie. "He has never signed up for military service, Sir."

"Vinnie, why haven't you?" the Captain asked.

"I did not know that I needed to," Vinnie replied, still not understanding quite what this was all about. "I just got my green card less than three weeks ago."

"You got your green card? What do you mean, your green card?" Now his friend was the one in the room who was puzzled.

Vinnie explained. "Yeah, I wasn't legal in the country until three weeks ago."

The Captain didn't hide the shock on his face. Sitting down in a chair, he scratched his head. "Are you telling me you haven't been legal all this time?"

"No," Vinnie said.

"WHY DIDN'T YOU TELL ME THAT?!" his friend shouted.

The answer was obvious to Vinnie. "You never asked me."

"You almost got a job working for the FBI and you weren't even legally in this country until just recently?!" The Captain still couldn't believe it.

"Yes. No one ever asked me if I was a citizen or not. There was no question on the application that I filled out about being a US citizen."

Vinnie's neighbor shook his head in disbelief and looked at the other man. His voice softened as he instructed the FBI officer. "Just tell him where to go."

Opening the door to leave, the Captain turned to Vinnie. "You almost got me in big trouble, Vinnie." Still shaking his head, Vinnie's friend and neighbor walked out of the room.

Vinnie was shaking his head too, as he left the FBI office and headed for home. Legalities and love, a man could pretty quickly get himself tangled up in both.

CHAPTER 21

Called by Uncle Sam

October 1960

Fort Dix, New Jersey

The letter came in the mail just a few weeks later. Vinnie had followed the FBI officer's instructions, going to the Flushing Army Recruiting Center and filled out his paperwork, signing up for the draft.

"Uncle Sam Wants You" the letter said, with a goofy-looking cartoon of an old bearded man wearing a crazy hat pointing his finger right at Vinnie. Vinnie gave notice to the school that he was leaving to serve in the Army and made arrangements with someone to store his beloved new convertible, paying him $200 for the two years he was going to be gone. Expecting that he may not have a chance to come back home before being shipped out, Vinnie packed a few pairs of clean underwear and socks, bid his family farewell, kissed Margaret good-bye, and reported as requested on October 26, 1960 at the downtown New York City Army headquarters where new recruits and draftees were processed. After giving Vinnie a physical and filling out the paperwork (always so much paperwork in America!), an Army officer walked from man to man talking with each one, sorting them according to how well they spoke English. With New York City being such a melting pot of cultures, men were of many different nationalities, some not able to speak any English at all.

When the man began asking him questions, Vinnie spoke up. "You know before I do this, I am not even a citizen," he told the officer.

"You want to live here, don't you?" the officer answered back.

"Well, yes," Vinnie replied.

"Then you will serve this country like everyone else!"

He pointed Vinnie toward the room on the right, and despite his nervousness at what his future in the Army would be, Vinnie couldn't help feeling just a little bit proud at that moment. He had apparently passed his first English "exam," as Vinnie was sent to join the group of recruits that spoke adequate English.

As he suspected, after the physicals were finished, the paperwork filled out, and the processing completed, Vinnie joined a bus full of recruits as they headed south for Basic Training with the US Army in Fort Dix, New Jersey.

Vinnie left New York City with mixed emotions. Of course, he hated leaving his new wife and the good life he'd made for himself. But, a part of him yearned to see more of this huge nation called the United States, and the adventurous side of him couldn't help but be a little bit excited at the yet unknown experiences that surely lay ahead.

Carrying a small duffle bag with the few personal items he'd brought from home, Vinnie walked down the steps of the bus after the four-hour ride from New York City. On the bus he'd made a few new friends, a couple of fellows from Long Island. Vinnie didn't know them, but it felt good to talk to people who had that much in common with him. Filing off the bus, the new recruits were taken to a big building where they waited for the completion of more paperwork before being led into a room where they were measured and issued seven sets of work clothing, shoes, and both summer and winter dress uniforms. From there, Vinnie followed the line into the barracks that he would share with 59 other young Army privates, home to their platoon for the next eight weeks of their lives.

Vinnie looked around the big room filled with 30 sets of bunk beds, 60 footlockers, and 60 narrow closet lockers. It was sparse but functional and immaculate. Off to the side of the entrance was a small room, his Sergeant's room. In the back was a large bathroom area, with toilets and open shower stalls. He couldn't help but remember his days on the ships, the tiny beds and miniature closets and bathrooms. At least in the Army, he had a little more room to stretch!

Laying his duffle bag onto the bottom bunk he was assigned, Vinnie did as instructed and got into line for a set of sheets, blanket, and pillow for the bed. After unpacking his meager belongings into his footlocker and hanging his Army-issued clothes in his closet, the Sergeant ordered them all to the front of the barracks. He was going to teach them how to make their beds.

"How hard can that be?" Vinnie thought, but soon found out that the Army could make even the seemingly simple task of bed-making quite complicated. Everything had to be folded and tucked just so, and the Sergeant demonstrated what a well-made bed should be like, taking a shiny quarter and bouncing it high off the taut blanket.

"You'll know your bed is made properly when you can bounce a quarter off it, just like that," the Sergeant told them. It may have looked easy, but as many times as Vinnie had made a bed in his life, getting one smooth and tight enough to bounce a quarter off like that was a challenge and took Vinnie several attempts to accomplish.

Vinnie soon learned the routine of Army life. At 5:00 a.m. the men fell out of their beds for reveille, awakened by the bugler. Throwing some clothes on, they assembled outside for the raising of and saluting to the flag, as well as a short briefing and instructions for the day from the Sergeant. Then, Vinnie and the others went back into the barracks, made their beds, used the latrine, showered, and dressed for the day. Everyone had an assignment to complete before falling into formation and marching to the Mess Hall for breakfast.

Lines, lines, lines...it seemed to Vinnie he was always waiting in a line. For every meal he stood in line, and years later Vinnie would refuse to stand in line at a restaurant because of his many years of standing in line to eat while he was in the Army.

Basic Training was eight weeks of hellish physical torture. Vinnie's small frame had managed to pack on some extra pounds in his years in America, and he was shocked himself when he weighed in at 260 pounds during his Army physical. But those pounds dropped off quickly and his Army pants got looser and looser as every day was filled from sun-up to sun-down with non-stop marching or running, calisthenics, several-mile marches carrying a forty-pound field pack on his back, and obstacle courses that pushed Vinnie and his buddies to the limit. Vinnie always seemed to be straggling near the back of the line, struggling to keep up. "Come on, Fatso!" Vinnie could hear the Sergeant yelling at him, but as rough as it was somehow Vinnie managed to keep on going. He might die trying, Vinnie often thought, but it just wasn't in him to ever give up. Never.

The Army managed to pack a whole lot of activity into eight weeks. The platoon spent days in the woods learning survival skills. Rifle training and target-shooting were new to Vinnie. He'd used his dad's shotgun before, but had never shot anything nearly as powerful as the Army weapons. Guns had never held much fascination for Vinnie, but he learned the skills required by the Army. And at least when he was shooting a gun, he didn't have to be doing that dreaded, constant marching.

At nights, especially in the early days of Basic Training, lying in the darkness of the barracks, his muscles aching from exhaustion and almost too tired to even sleep, Vinnie could hear the stifled sobs of men crying in the bunks. Most of these young men had never been away from the comfort and easy life of their homes, and the Army proved to be a rude awakening. Sergeant would walk through the bunks, chiding them, "What's wrong with you guys?! Are you missing your mommies?"

Vinnie, having been gone from home for eight years now, was not among the weepers. He'd gotten over missing his family a long time ago. Not that he didn't wish he could see them, he did. But he was a man now, and men didn't cry for their mommies. What he did miss was his New York life, the cozy home and young wife he'd left behind. Had it only been just a few weeks? It seemed like another world ago.

Six weeks into Basic Training, Vinnie was fortunate enough to be included in the half of the men from his platoon who were issued a long weekend pass. He was so excited! His first opportunity to go back home to Long Island, he called Margaret to let her know he was coming, and smiled his way through the rest of the agonizingly long days knowing he'd been sleeping in his own bed before the week's end. On Friday afternoon he bought a bus ticket and headed for home. Margaret was thrilled to see him! The three days flew by way too quickly before it was time to leave Long Island once more, and his brother-in-law drove him back to Fort Dix.

Revived after some time away and with only two weeks of training to go, Vinnie knew he was on the home stretch. The very worst part of being drafted into the army was nearly over, then things would surely take a more pleasant turn. The next week went by quickly, and when Friday morning's formation rolled around something quite unexpected happened.

"I need six volunteers to clean the Colonel's office," the First Sergeant told his men. "Who will volunteer?"

Vinnie, knowing he'd be stuck at the base anyway since he'd already had his three-day pass home and thinking cleaning the

Colonel's office would be a whole lot better than some other detail to which he could be assigned, raised his hand. It hadn't taken Vinnie and his buddies long to realize it usually isn't wise to volunteer in the Army, but he decided to go with his gut feeling and do it just this once. Cleaning the office shouldn't take too long, and then he'd have some free time on his hands to hang around the barracks and relax some over the weekend.

Seeing Vinnie's as the only hand raised, First Sergeant repeated his request. "I want five more people who will volunteer to clean the Colonel's office." Silence. And only Vinnie's hand was up.

"Nerich, put your hand down." First Sergeant sighed loudly in annoyance, turned around and waited a few moments, then faced his platoon again. "Now I'm going to ask one more time...I need six volunteers to go clean the Colonel's office before we will issue three-day passes. Step out."

Vinnie stepped two paces out in front of the line. One more fellow did the same, two of them stepping out of line to volunteer. "No one else willing to do it?" First Sergeant asked sternly, clearly aggravated. No one moved.

First Sergeant turned around to the officer behind him, a Lieutenant. "Sir, give these two men three-day passes." Then turning to face the other soldiers, picking out men randomly with his pointing finger, "You, you, you...go clean the Colonel's office!" And he marched away.

Vinnie, although thrilled about another three-day pass, paid his dues for the privilege, as the rest of the men in his platoon gave him a very hard time for being so obliging. This time no one expected Vinnie when he arrived home for the second weekend in a row. He was a little disappointed to walk into his empty home after he got off the bus, since his wife was still at work. But nevertheless, Vinnie certainly enjoyed his surprise weekend back in Long Island.

His volunteering spirit back-fired later, and Vinnie learned a valuable lesson for surviving in the Army. Never volunteer. One day during formation, Sergeant asked the men, "Does anyone have his driver's license?" Obviously nearly every man in the platoon had a driver's license, but Vinnie and just a few others raised their hands.

"Report to the motor pool," he was ordered, and Vinnie and the others did just that.

"Let me see your driver's license," the motor pool Sergeant asked. Vinnie obliged, pulling it out and showing it to him.

The officer nodded. "See that wheelbarrow over there? I want you to drive it over to that pile of debris, load it up and haul it away."

After spending the day driving the wheelbarrow, Vinnie had learned his lesson. Never volunteer in the Army.

It would have been impossible for Vinnie to spend eight weeks without pulling some sort of a prank, and once he and a few buddies got the whole platoon in trouble. Seeing some whistling fireworks in the PX one day, Vinnie joked that it would be funny to attach one to the spark plug under the hood of First Sergeant's car. The buddies that were with Vinnie upped the ante a little, and it was the Lieutenant's car that eventually got rigged with the little explosive. When the unaware Lieutenant started his car, the men tried to stifle their laughter when they heard shrill whistling as smoke poured out from under the hood and Lieutenant jumped out of the car as fast as he could and ran, thinking his car was on fire and about to explode.

Soon realizing it was a prank, Lieutenant's fear turned to anger as he walked over to his men and called them together. "I want to know who did this!" he demanded.

This time Vinnie was certainly NOT going to raise his hand, and neither were his co-conspirators. Everyone did his best to act innocent and look surprised. "WHO DID THIS???!!!"

Silence. Most of the men in the company actually were

innocent, no one having any knowledge about the joke except Vinnie and his few close buddies. The soldiers kept staring ahead, no one willing to own up to the prank nor rat on his fellow pranksters.

"Start running!" Lieutenant ordered.

And the men dropped the tasks they were doing and hit the trail. For the next two hours at least, they ran, boots and all, until the whole company was about to collapse, all the while thinking and muttering under their breath, "I'm gonna kill the guys to blame for this!" Vinnie joined in, "Who would be so stupid to do such a thing?" hoping no one would ever discover that he was involved.

Out of breath and their legs rubbery, the men were finally ordered to stop running. "I'm going to ask you again, who did it?" Lieutenant demanded. Silence, except for the panting of the tired men. No one dared breathe a word.

For the next several days, the entire platoon was restricted to the barracks, only allowed to leave to go to the Mess Hall and even then having to be escorted like a bunch of schoolboys by the Sergeant. Inside the barracks, the normal chatter and laughter was hushed. Being careful to stay out of earshot from the officers, the men whispered, "Sure wish we could find out who played that prank on the Lieutenant." Vinnie convinced them that it must have been the platoon upstairs that did it, certainly not any of them. Those involved didn't dare mention anything to the others, all of them playing dumb and acting as innocent as anyone else.

No one ever confessed nor did anyone squeal. Much later Vinnie would laugh as he related the incident, but at the time there was no one laughing... at least not on the outside.

CHAPTER 22

Private Nerich

1961

Fort Leonard Wood, Missouri

Two whole weeks of freedom! No reveille, no ceaseless running, no marching, no standing in lines, no one ordering him around...Vinnie had fourteen days from the end of Basic Training to his required reporting for duty at his next assignment in Fort Leonard Wood, Missouri.

Riding the bus from Fort Dix back to Long Island, Vinnie watched the rural landscapes turn into suburbia then into city blocks blurring past his window, and he felt proud. His overweight body from eight weeks ago was now sleek and toned, in better physical shape than he'd ever been in his life. Despite the harsh regimen and brutal physical challenges, he'd survived Basic Training just fine.

The last few days before he left Fort Dix, all the men had taken an aptitude skill test to help determine where they should be assigned. Vinnie, although by now able to communicate in English with his peers, still could not read or write in English. He hoped the officers administering the test wouldn't notice his heart practically thumping out of his chest as they handed him the paper and pencil. Knowing there was no way he'd be able to read the test and complete it on time, he began guessing, coloring the circles in randomly. At least on the true/false portion he had a fifty-fifty chance of answering correctly. The multiple choice were a little more worrisome, but Vinnie had a plan. Writing on tiny slips of paper "A," "B," "C," and "D," he threw them in his hat and said a little prayer. For each question he drew out a slip at random, using that answer and leaving it up to God to direct his hand. Needing a score of 57% or higher, Vinnie was elated to score 61% and so was directed to the skill area that interested him most anyway. Vinnie was going to train to be a mechanic.

Margaret appeared glad enough to have him home, although Vinnie sensed something was just not quite right. He couldn't quite put his finger on it, but his wife seemed a little distant. Vinnie brushed it off, thinking she just needed to get used to having him around again, and enjoyed his days at home, visiting Nick and his family and catching up with his neighborhood friends. Eight weeks didn't look that long on a calendar, but Vinnie felt like his whole world had changed drastically in just eight short weeks.

Bidding his family good-bye once again, this time the bus Vinnie boarded was heading west, west to Missouri. Looking out the bus windows, this was part of America that Vinnie had yet to see. Acres and acres with no houses, miles and miles between towns, Vinnie was in brand new territory. The vacant farm fields were brown and crusted with snow, stretching out endlessly on the other side of his Greyhound window.

After traveling for several hours, the bus driver pulled in at a truck stop somewhere in northern Indiana. Vinnie followed the other passengers off, some of them military and some civilian, walking toward the building to use the restrooms and get a bite to eat. As he walked by wearing his Army uniform, he passed a lady. "Good morning, Soldier! How are you this morning?" she smiled and asked. Vinnie, stunned at being spoken to by a total stranger, answered. Just a few minutes later another stranger, this time a man, came up and shook his hand and started a friendly conversation with Vinnie. When the man had left, Vinnie turned around to the bus driver, who was in line behind him.

"Are we still in the United States?" Vinnie asked the driver.

The bus driver was puzzled. "Well, yes. Why?"

Vinnie was equally puzzled. "These people are so friendly here!" Having become accustomed to the cold haughty attitudes he found in New York City and New Jersey, Vinnie had assumed that's how Americans acted. That had been one thing that had shocked Vinnie when he'd first arrived from Yugoslavia. Where he was reared, the villagers all knew each other and were friendly and happy to see you. He'd found a stark contrast with New Yorkers. The few times he'd asked someone on the street for directions or help, they'd either ignored him and kept on walking or, even worse, intentionally lied to him. The only people Vinnie found to be sincerely helpful in New York City were policemen or mailmen, and even they were not exactly friendly but at least Vinnie could count on them to give him a truthful answer. Nasty unhappy folks, Vinnie had thought more than once about most of the city people with whom he had come in contact.

Laughing, the bus driver told Vinnie, "The further west you go, young man, the friendlier people get."

Getting back on the Greyhound, Vinnie traveled on the bus several more hours before arriving in St. Louis. Vinnie checked in at the Army Recruiting Center where an officer reviewed his paperwork and directed him to a waiting area where he sat with other soldiers for another five hours before boarding an Army bus with its destination Fort Leonard Wood. Vinnie was thankful to have with him another fellow from his Basic Training with the same MOS (Military Occupational Specialty, a code assigned to each soldier depending on his skill area) as him, the two of them both on their way to becoming Army mechanics.

Arriving at Fort Leonard Wood, Vinnie was excited to put the tough physical training behind him and learn a real trade in the Army, skills he could use to make a living for himself and his family after his Army days were over. For the next eight weeks, called "The Second Eight," Vinnie would go to mechanic school, part of the time in the classroom and part of the time in the shop. He learned to change tires, change the oil, how to work on military vehicles, and such. After learning the basics, the instructors would intentionally take something apart under the hood and the mechanics-in-training would have to trouble-shoot and fix the problem. Vinnie had worked part-time for a while at a gas station in New York, so he had a little knowledge of cars, but military vehicles were much different and required a whole new set of skills, and he was eager to take on the challenge.

An enthusiastic learner, Vinnie caught on quickly. He'd always enjoyed tinkering with things, figuring out how they work, and he was a quick problem-solver. Being a mechanic fit well with Vinnie's natural abilities, and it seemed to Vinnie that God and the Army had led him into the vocation perfectly suited for him.

Vinnie also worked with a civilian company of engineers employed by the Army. This company had a lot of big earth-moving machinery, bulldozers, backhoes, and other heavy equipment. Vinnie found out quickly how little he really knew about such vehicles when he opened his mouth one day.

"I could probably drive any piece of equipment out here," Vinnie prematurely boasted to one of the civilian engineers.

A smirk tickling the edges of his mouth, the engineer replied. "You can, huh? See that bulldozer over there?" Vinnie nodded. "Go start it up."

Feeling pretty sure that he could most certainly get the bulldozer started, Vinnie strode confidently across the lot, looked over the monstrous machine with giant tracks and the huge blade on front, and climbed up into the seat. Sitting atop the gigantic contraption, he felt pretty small, and it took only a moment for Vinnie to realize that perhaps he had bitten off more than he could chew. The bulldozer had no steering wheel, just a lot of levers in front and around him.

Vinnie tried to start it. No go. He looked around at all the gears and levers and tried everything he could think of but nothing worked. Glancing back at the group of watching engineers, Vinnie felt his face go red, as it was easy to see they were all laughing at him. He turned back to his dilemma, trying and trying again to get the machine going, but the engine wouldn't even turn over.

The engineer finally walked over, looking up at the frustrated and embarrassed Vinnie sitting in the seat. "Having a little trouble, Nerich?" He grinned. "Before you can start this big brute you've got to start the pony engine over on the side to get it going," pointing to a small engine to the right of where Vinnie was sitting.

Sheepishly Vinnie cranked up the pony engine and then was finally able to get the diesel started. The engineer stepped back and watched. Vinnie, regaining his confidence now that he had the monster going, played with the levers a little figuring out which one did what, and started moving forward. But he forgot one crucial thing... he didn't raise the blade. Before Vinnie even knew what was happening, a huge mountain of dirt was piling up in front of him! Frantic, Vinnie looked to the group of engineers, who were waving their arms and yelling instructions that he couldn't hear over the roar of the powerful diesel engine. Pulling levers up and down, right and left, forward and back, Vinnie was desperately trying to get the massive machine under control before he hit a building or fell down the steep drop-off to the side. Finally, in desperation, Vinnie just let go of the levers for a second and the machine stopped. For the rest of his time in mechanics' school, no one let Vinnie forget that incident. And Vinnie learned to be a little more careful when he opened his mouth!

The Second Eight was not nearly as strict and draining as Basic, and on weekends Vinnie and his buddies had their days free to go anywhere they wished within a fifty-mile radius of Fort Leonard Wood. Located just at the edge of the Ozarks, it was beautiful country and sometimes they'd go explore caves. Not too far away from the base was Ricetown, a community made up of bars, prostitutes, and tattoo parlors that catered to military men. Vinnie enjoyed going to the Biergarten and drinking 10-cent bottles of beer with his friends, and during Happy Hour they only had to pay five cents. Once, several of them had plans to get a tattoo, and Vinnie was paging through the designs waiting his turn in the tattoo parlor. Contemplating getting an Army insignia on his upper arm, Vinnie asked the tattoo artist how much it would cost. "Twenty-five dollars," the man answered.

"Twenty-five dollars???" Vinnie was shocked. "Do you know how many beers we can buy for twenty-five dollars? Let's get out of here!" And Vinnie left, never getting a tattoo.

Vinnie quickly and easily made friends with both his Army compatriots and the civilians who worked at Fort Leonard Wood. People were attracted to his friendly smile and his funny accent, and enjoyed hearing stories about his home country Yugoslavia. More weekends than not, one of his civilian friends would invite Vinnie to spend his days off with his family, picking Vinnie up and taking him home for a couple of nights.

It was during his weeks at Fort Leonard Wood that Vinnie had his first hillbilly experience. One of his Army friends, Moore, was from Arkansas and invited Vinnie to go home with him on a three-day leave. Getting special permission, since it was beyond the fifty-mile radius, Moore had told Vinnie that he lived out in the country, nothing fancy. Vinnie cared nothing at all about that as long as he could get a break from Army life and get some good home cooking. Once he got off the main highway, Moore drove and drove, miles and miles onto narrower and narrower country roads, finally pulling up an overgrown gravel driveway to a little ramshackle wooden house sitting on the side of a hill. The front porch was propped up with stacked cement blocks, and a hound dog picked up its lazy bones and wagged its tail over to greet them.

The Moores were friendly folk, Mr. Moore wearing his big overalls rolled up at the ankle showing his dirty bare feet. The whole family went barefoot, inside and out. Moore lent Vinnie some old clothes and shoes, handed him a gun belt holding a 22-gauge pistol, and told him they were going out to shoot their supper. They brought home a rattlesnake, a couple of rabbits, and three or four frogs that afternoon, and Moore's momma cooked them up and served them for supper accompanied by all kinds of home-grown vegetables. Not a single thing on the table had come from a grocery store.

Mr. Moore was a joker, always trying to pull one over on the young friends Moore brought home. "Betcha ain't gonna eat that rattlesnake, are ya?" he chided Vinnie as he forked a piece onto Vinnie's plate. Vinnie looked straight in the elder Moore's eyes as he popped a morsel into his mouth. Mr. Moore didn't realize he was dealing with a young man who grew up on raw sardines and octopus. The white meat of the boiled and skinned rattlesnake had a striking resemblance to the moray eel meat that was a staple in the Njiric home back in Yugoslavia, and eating the snake Vinnie felt a brief wave of homesickness sweep over him.

"It's good," Vinnie said. "I'd like some more."

With a nearly-toothless grin, Mr. Moore said, "No, no...you cain't have no more. I want some too."

After supper, Mr. Moore had another challenge. "You a drinkin' man?" When Vinnie answered that yes, he drank once in a while, Mr. Moore led him out to a shack of a barn. Vinnie followed him across the wooden floor over to the corner, where Mr. Moore kicked a bunch of straw away and opened a trap door in the floor.

Reaching down below, Mr. Moore hauled out a jug of moonshine.

"Here's how we drink around these parts," Mr. Moore demonstrated, looping his thumb through the handle and tipping the ceramic jug over his shoulder, letting the moonshine trickle into his mouth.

Vinnie'd tasted his share of Croatian moonshine over the years, so he didn't hesitate when Mr. Moore handed him the jug. But even Vinnie had to admit, this was strong stuff! His eyes and mouth burned, but Vinnie swallowed a couple of times. "It's pretty good," he said, and he could tell Mr. Moore was pleased.

"You'll try anything, won't ya?" as he grinned his nearly-toothless grin, and Vinnie knew he had made himself a new hillbilly friend.

Moore drove Vinnie into the nearest little town, Wind, a crossroads community full of rusty pick-ups, beat-up cars, and gun-toting folks. It wasn't often that the townspeople in Wind saw a stranger in town, and the people were very friendly. For the most part. Vinnie did find himself facing one drunk, jealous fellow when Vinnie, urged on by Moore, innocently asked a young woman sitting along the outskirts of the dance floor to be his dance partner. Apparently she wasn't in the bar alone, and her man didn't take too kindly to a stranger trying to pick up his girlfriend and tried to start a fight, but Vinnie quickly backed away and got out of there in time.

The eight weeks in Fort Leonard Wood flew by much more quickly than those first eight weeks in Basic, and when his time there was almost up, Vinnie and the other men were asked to choose where they would like to be stationed next. Vinnie's friend, whom he'd been with since Basic Training, chose Europe. Not wanting to go back to Europe yet and hoping it might expedite his citizenship process, Vinnie chose Korea or Vietnam as his preference. When soldiers were sent into a war zone, citizenship was automatic and Vinnie was willing to do anything, including combat in a war zone, to hold those precious citizenship papers in his hand.

When the assignments were made, Vinnie was astonished to learn that he was going to Europe and his friend to Korea, just the opposite of what the two of them had requested. So Vinnie went to the First Sergeant, an old fellow who Vinnie figured must have been in the Army for fifty years, and asked him about it. "Son, you're in the Army now. Whatever you ask for, they'll give you the opposite. If you want to go to the PX, they'll send you to the EM club. Everything in the Army is always backwards."

And so Vinnie received his orders to go to Germany. Buying a bus ticket, he used his time between orders to go home to New York for a few days. It was nice to see Margaret again after two months away, but Vinnie couldn't shake the feeling that things between them were just not quite the same. Being sent to Europe, Vinnie knew it'd be a long time before they saw each other again, and when Vinnie kissed Margaret good-bye, he had no idea that it'd be the last time he would ever see her.

Vinnie reported as ordered to a port along the New York coastline, boarded a ship, and couldn't help feeling sad and disappointed. Watching New York City fade in the distance as the ship sailed away, he remembered how excited he'd been when he'd seen that same city grow larger as he'd watched from the *Andrea Doria* five years ago. Vinnie wasn't ready to go back to Europe, but he had no choice. He was in the Army now.

CHAPTER 23

AWOL

Summer 1961

Europe

Seasickness hit nearly everyone onboard, as the ship encountered rough waters crossing the Atlantic. All around him, Vinnie watched men's faces turn green, groaning and vomiting. Vinnie wasn't affected in the least, having spent nearly his entire life on the sea. He found himself amused that a little choppy water could so easily rattle these tough military guys, and kind of enjoyed flaunting his tough stomach by eating in front of them and nauseating them even more.

Porting in Germany, each soldier was handed a computer punch-card as they disembarked. Computers were the newest technology, and the punch-card became the Army's new improved paperwork system. As Vinnie was doing his punch-through, the officer in charge directed him to wait with the group that was being sent to France.

Vinnie shrugged his shoulders. Germany, France, Italy...what difference did it make to him? He didn't want to be in Europe at all. Along with his group of other France-bound soldiers, Vinnie boarded a train sending him southwest to France. Getting off the train and walking into the office there with his punch-card in hand, Vinnie saluted the Army officer. "Reporting for duty, Sir."

The officer looked at the card and then back up at Vinnie. "Where did you take your training, Private Nerich?"

"Fort Leonard Wood, Missouri, Sir."

"The Army doesn't have any locomotive training in Fort Leonard Wood," the officer replied.

Locomotive? "The only locomotive I know about, Sir, is the New York City subway. I've had no training for locomotives."

"Your paperwork says you are a locomotive operator," said the officer. Vinnie told the officer that his MOS was for a mechanic, and they soon figured out what had happened. In punching in Vinnie's MOS, a mistake had been made on the last letter in the code...the difference between being a designated as a locomotive operator or a mechanic.

Realizing the mistake, Vinnie was ordered to go work in the motor pool. So Vinnie was assigned to the night shift of the Army's 77th Transportation squad, working from 6:00 p.m. to 6:00 a.m., hours he was familiar with from his *Andrea Doria* baking days. My, how long ago those days seemed!

Vinnie thought things were going fine and he was beginning to settle into Army life in France. He had written Margaret to give her his new address, and he loved getting a letter from her every couple of weeks. The first paycheck he got was only $12.50 for the month, but he didn't worry a whole lot about it, figuring he was only getting paid for part of a month and the Army was sending a large portion of his pay home. But when the second month's paycheck was also only $12.50, Vinnie wondered why he was only receiving partial pay. Knowing it was best not to question the Army's ways, this time Vinnie kept his mouth shut.

Unbeknownst to Vinnie, all of his official paperwork had been sent to Germany. All the while that Vinnie was working in the motor pool at the base in France, the Army base in Germany was reporting him as AWOL since he had never officially reported for duty there. It took six months for the paperwork to be processed through the Pentagon and catch up with him, and Vinnie was astonished when his commanding officer one day informed him that he was AWOL in Germany.

So it was in autumn of 1961 that Vinnie was sent back to Germany, this time on a delivery truck instead of a train. The convoy left from La Rochelle, stopping in Nancy, France to spend the night before arriving the next day in Frankfurt, Germany where the main Army dispatch office was located. The two-story building was large and spacious, with big open staircases leading to the second floor. Walking over to the main desk, Vinnie showed his paperwork to the recruiting officer, who told Vinnie he would send someone to pick him up. Standing on the first floor waiting for his ride, Vinnie watched through the wall of windows at the staircase leading to the street level above.

"Private Nerich!" His name echoed down the staircase and into the huge open room. Vinnie turned to see an Army guy standing at the top of the stairs. "Get your stuff and come with me." The man walked down the stairs, picked up one of Vinnie's duffle bags, and Vinnie followed him back up the stairs, out the door, and into the Army jeep.

Shaking Vinnie's hand, the man introduced himself. "My name is David." Vinnie didn't catch his last name, but the two chatted as David drove him to the base headquarters. David was one of the Colonel's drivers, and had been sent to pick Vinnie up that day. David also was the one responsible to deliver the payroll, accompanied by two armed guards since the Army pay was in cash at that time. Just having delivered that day's payroll, when he'd gone to the office to turn in the gun that he carried while doing that task, Dave (as he'd told Vinnie to call him) had been given orders to go pick up the AWOL soldier who was arriving from France.

Vinnie and Dave immediately hit it off, becoming friends from that very first encounter. Dave Catron (Vinnie later learned his last name) talked to the First Sergeant and arranged for Vinnie to be put in the same room with him and his four other roommates. Obviously, Dave had a lot of influence at the base, highly regarded and trusted by the higher-ups. Vinnie had lucked into finding a great friend his very first hours in Germany!

The next morning, Vinnie reported for duty to the motor pool officer, Sergeant Fox. Sergeant Fox bore an uncanny resemblance to the animal, wearing his hat down his pointy nose and peering intently at Vinnie with sharp, beady eyes from beneath its brim. Irritated that Private Nerich hadn't arrived a long time ago when he'd been expected, as soon as Vinnie saluted and reported for duty, Sergeant Fox held out the keys.

"Private Nerich. Here are the keys. I'm going on leave and you are in charge." And without any further instruction, he dropped the ring of keys into Vinnie's hand, turned his back, and walked away. Vinnie was stunned! He had no idea what to do with the keys and command that had just been handed over to him, and Vinnie stared dumbfounded at Sergeant Fox's back as he walked away.

And so, on his very first day of duty in Germany, Vinnie found himself in charge of the base's motor pool. He was the mechanic, the parts orderer, the dispatcher, the bookkeeper, anything and everything that had to do with running the motor pool. He had no idea where to even begin! Vinnie was very grateful for his new friend Dave, who helped him figure things out. Being the Colonel's driver, Dave reported to the motor pool every morning for his day's trip tickets. Every time a military vehicle was used, the drivers kept a complete record of the date, time, miles driven, starting point and destination for each trip, how long it took, every minute detail recorded meticulously, and the ticket was turned back in with the vehicle to the motor pool at the end of the day to be recorded by

Vinnie in the log book.

Dave showed him how things worked. The two most important daily duties were dispatching the Army bus to pick up the officers from their homes and transport them to Headquarters and dispatching Dave to drive the car to pick up the Colonel and take him to Headquarters. Those were Vinnie's first jobs every morning. Between help from the bus driver and Dave, Vinnie learned how to fill out the required paperwork and send the bus and Colonel's car out each morning. Little by little, Vinnie learned the ropes and before long he was running the motor pool like he'd done it his entire life.

Vinnie wrote Margaret a letter, telling her about the whole AWOL mix-up and letting her know he was now in Germany, and it looked like he was going to stay there for a while. He thought it odd that he never received an answer back. In fact, come to think of it, he hadn't heard from his wife for several weeks now. After the first two or three months while he was in France, the letters from home became less and less frequent, more time passing between each one until finally they had stopped coming. Vinnie assumed that the letters had been going to France and hadn't been forwarded to him after his transfer to Germany, but when he never received a response when he'd been in Germany for a few weeks, Vinnie knew something was wrong.

Ever since he'd been in the Army, a large chunk of his pay was automatically sent to his wife back home. By this time, Vinnie was making $110 a month; $75 of it was being sent back as an allotment to Margaret, with Vinnie's share being just $35. At first, he wasn't bothered at all by this. She was his wife, and he was responsible for supporting her. But as time went on and he never heard from Margaret, Vinnie finally asked his friend at Headquarters if he might get some help to find out what was going on back home. The officer got the American Red Cross involved, hoping they could investigate the situation. A short while later, Vinnie was told that the Red Cross could not locate Margaret; she was no longer living in New York.

Vinnie was puzzled and mad, as well as very frustrated. The Army checks were being cashed regularly, but where was his wife? Headquarters issued Vinnie a thirty-day emergency leave for Vinnie to go home and take care of his personal affairs, so he flew to New York City and stopped by their apartment. Another renter was living in his home with no sign of his wife or their belongings. Angry and confused, Vinnie paid a visit to Margaret's mother who claimed she had no idea where her daughter was, that she'd sold everything (including Vinnie's Chevy convertible) and took off with a truck driver from out west.

Vinnie's mother-in-law had been cashing the checks all this time! Whether Margaret was getting any of the money, Vinnie had no idea. He just knew he needed to find his wife and put an end to their charade of a marriage.

While he was home in New York, Margaret's mother sent Vinnie a message. Apparently her daughter had called, and the mother had told her that Vinnie was home trying to find her. Margaret gave a message for her mother to relay to Vinnie: if he wanted her back, Vinnie was to place a personal ad on a specified page in the New York Times newspaper. So that's what Vinnie did, going into the newspaper's office in downtown New York City, paying $15 to submit a personal ad telling her he wanted her back, included a phone number where she could contact him, and waited for her reply. Day after day passed with no phone call, no answer, nothing. Soon his thirty days were up, and Vinnie had to go back to Germany without ever having heard from his wife.

Feeling like the entire thirty days was a total waste of Vinnie's time and money, he reported back to Germany frustrated and disappointed. He knew his marriage was over.

After further investigation, the Army did discover that Margaret's mother was indeed cashing the checks illegally. Vinnie was asked if he wanted to press charges but he declined, seeing no sense in prolonging the whole ordeal. Ready to put it behind him and move on, Vinnie filed the necessary paperwork to stop the allotment.

Vinnie hadn't been back in Germany very long when he did get a phone call, a strange one from a man claiming to be Margaret's doctor from Long Island and asking Vinnie to send money. When the man refused to let Vinnie speak to his wife, Vinnie told him he was not sending any money and hung up the telephone.

Then about a month later, when the paperwork finally went through and the allotments stopped coming, Margaret's mother contacted the Army in a fury, saying she needed that money to take care of her daughter. When he found out, Vinnie called Margaret's mother one last time. Not able to get a straight answer about his wife's whereabouts, Vinnie told her, "Next time you talk to your daughter tell her to call me," giving his mother-in-law his phone number and the best time to reach him.

That was the last time Vinnie ever heard from them. Margaret never called and her mother gave up trying to get back the Army allotment. He may have still legally been married, but his marriage was finished.

Vinnie hadn't really been AWOL, but he sure couldn't say the same about his wife.

CHAPTER 24

"You're in the Army Now"

1961-1964

Frankfurt, Germany

Winnie. Fond of his new nickname, it reminded Vinnie of the cuddly, cute, sweet cartoon bear Winnie-the-Pooh that he'd seen Niko's children watch on television.

He came to be called Winnie by accident. The Germans had trouble pronouncing his name because their language does not have a "v" sound, so when they spoke his name it came out "Winnie" instead of "Vinnie." That was okay by him. It wasn't the first time he'd gone by a different name, and it amused Winnie to hear his name as part of the lyrics of a children's song about Pooh, sung in German, *"Winnie, Winnie, wonder, wander..."* that his friends chimed in singing when he was around. And so the name "Winnie" stuck, and Vinnie didn't mind it at all.

Finally having put his disastrous marriage behind him, Winnie felt like a weight had been lifted off his shoulders. He hadn't really felt ready to get married to begin with and he knew in his heart from the very beginning that Margaret was not the woman with whom God intended for him to spend the rest of his days.

It took a while to heal his broken heart, but Winnie was glad to get his personal life back on track and enjoyed his time in Germany so much that he and Dave both decided to re-enlist when their first two years were finished. Winnie bought Sergeant Fox's car when, not long after returning from his vacation, the sergeant was reassigned to another job. Winnie had become well acquainted with Sergeant Fox's 1953 Chevy, having worked on it many times when the car broke down. One night when he and Dave were hanging out together having a few drinks in the club, Sergeant Fox came up to Winnie, told him he was leaving to go back to the States, and wondered if Winnie might like to buy his car. "Sure," Winnie told him, "but I don't have any money to buy a car."

"Give me a dollar," Sergeant Fox said, and after Winnie pulled a dollar out of his pocket, Sergeant Fox pulled out the car title and signed it over to Winnie right then and there. The car needed a lot of work, but the price was right and Winnie enjoyed tinkering with it in his free time. Dave also had a small car, which he traded in for a big Bonneville convertible, and the two of them had a grand old time driving through Frankfurt after forty straight days of snowfall, maneuvering the snow-piled streets with the convertible top down.

The Army base at Frankfurt, just a couple of blocks from the train station, was like a city in itself. Surrounded by a circle of walls with just two large gated and guarded entrances opposite each other, inside the casern was everything Winnie and his buddies needed. With a grid of streets connecting the buildings, there was a PX, a bowling alley, a jail, the engineers' motor pool, the transportation motor pool, the military police motor pool, the MP station, the intelligence office, and several barracks inside. The casern where Winnie lived with Dave and his other buddies was really its own little community.

Winnie worked in the transportation motor pool, along the back wall of the casern, and the office had one window about eight feet up the twelve-foot walls overlooking the street outside. The window let light inside the room, but it was much too high to be able to see out. Winnie hung an angled mirror up by the window just so that he and his friends could watch the people walk by outside, especially the pretty German girls. Once during an inspection, a Colonel asked him why the mirror was there. "Sir," Winnie answered, "so we can check the traffic situation before we leave," and his answer satisfied the officer.

But Winnie wasn't about to stay confined in the casern. Outside those walls was real life, a bustling city with good food, great beer, and beautiful women. With Dave's clout, Winnie was usually able to easily get passes out of the casern, and the two of them would walk across the street to hang out at a joint called The Silver Bar run by a Jewish man and his daughter. Winnie and Dave's room was on the third floor of the casern, and on the other side of the casern wall right across from them were some houses and small shops, bars, and cafes. On occasion when the base was on lock-down for some sort of alert, and no one was allowed to leave, Winnie and Dave would holler out their window to the lady running the café across the street. Using a rope, they would lower a basket with money inside, pulling it back up after she had obliged and traded their money for beer and wiener schnitzels (a German favorite much like a tenderloin). Other times when they were not supposed to leave, since Winnie had befriended most of the guards through his job at the motor pool, he was able to persuade the guard on duty to let him just quickly run across the street for a beer or two even during an alert. Of course, both Winnie and the guard would have gotten into serious trouble had they been caught, but Winnie was smart and avoided trouble, at least most of the time.

Winnie hadn't been in Germany too long when his paperwork from the France/Germany AWOL mix-up finally got straightened out, and he was very pleasantly surprised to find back pay from his time in France added onto his paycheck. Six months of being paid only a part-time salary of $12.50 per month, Winnie received a nice sum of unexpected money on top of what he was normally due on his first payday in Germany, which happened to fall two weeks right before Christmas, a time when all the other soldiers were broke. Dave had pulled a few strings and managed to finagle a weekend-pass into Winnie's hands before his mandatory 30-day curfew for soldiers new to the base was over, and Winnie and his buddies had themselves a good old time on the town courtesy of Winnie's very timely windfall.

Working in the motor pool had its benefits, as Winnie made friendships with soldiers in all parts of the casern. The soldier who ran the arms room where the guns were kept and the fellow from the supply room became good friends of Winnie and Dave's. The four of them—Winnie, Dave, Bryant, and a guy named Dean Martin—had lots of fun hanging out together. Once they went to the civilian section of the Frankfurt airport to kill a few hours, and just for fun Winnie, Dave, and Bryant went to the Information Desk and asked the clerk there to please page Dean Martin to come to the desk. What a kick the men got when they heard the clerk doing just that, paging Dean Martin over the loudspeaker, and star-struck giggly girls appeared from all corners of the airport to see Dean Martin nonchalantly walk up, only to be disappointed that he wasn't exactly the famous Dean Martin that they were hoping to see.

During his tenure in Germany, Winnie did several other Army jobs besides running the transportation motor pool. As a wrecker-operator for the base Military Police, Winnie would go pick up broken-down or accident-damaged vehicles, both military and personal cars belonging to the military men, from the Autobahn and haul them back to the base for repair.

Being an automobile expert had its perks too, as Winnie was often given opportunities to earn some extra money on the side. Officers would pay him to wash the exteriors and clean up the interiors of their cars, and Winnie found it profitable to keep the loose change he found under the seats, which at times was considerable. The Colonel's wife had a big Buick convertible that she rarely drove, and when she did she never went faster than 35 mph, causing her big

4-barrel carburetor to get gummed up inside. The Colonel would hire Winnie to take the convertible out onto the Autobahn and run it hard and fast to blow the carbon out and clean out the carburetor. In fact, Winnie probably would have gladly done the job for free, as there was surely nothing much more exciting and fun for the young man than flying down the left lane of the Autobahn as fast as he could go in a flashy convertible. Even going over 100 mph, as there is no speed limit on the Autobahn, there always seemed to be a Ferrari or Porsche on his bumper eager to pass him going even faster. It was a "tough" job, but somebody had to do it!

Never one to sit still for long, Winnie was always one of the first soldiers on the club dance floor on the weekend nights, and quickly picked up a lot of dance moves that helped him pick up a lot of dance partners. German girls, Winnie discovered, loved two things: eating *pommes frites* (French fries) and dancing. Buy a German girl a plate of fries and whirl her around on the dance floor, and she was one happy gal. Jiggling his body to *"Wipe-Out"* pretty much won them over, and Winnie seldom found himself without an eager partner with whom to practice his shimmy-shimmy moves.

Laughing and dancing, Winnie was the life of the club parties; he enjoyed every minute of it, even entering dance contests at the club when he had the chance. Winning a couple of those contests, Winnie and his partner of the night received prize money and a trophy, and Winnie was pleased that the women were satisfied to keep the trophy and Winnie kept the prize money, the perfect split.

Pranks were a part of soldier life, and Winnie never shied away from a chance to pull one over on someone, especially a green young recruit who'd just been assigned to the base. If the company commander, the Captain, happened to be gone for the day, Winnie or Dave would get a big kick out of putting on the Captain's barred jacket and sitting behind his desk, pretending to be the Captain, and call for the new recruit. Already nervous and now having to meet with the man he thought was the Captain, Winnie would ask the young man how much money he had and offer to bend the rules, so he could leave the casern if the new soldier would buy drinks for everyone. Not feeling he had much choice, the new soldier always agreed and Winnie or Dave had bought themselves another free evening of fun. Thankfully for them, the two friends never got caught for that charade.

Oktoberfest was a huge deal in Germany, a three-day holiday that shut down the businesses and closed down the streets, a festival that the German people eagerly anticipated every autumn. Winnie and his buddies bought a few tiny whistling firecrackers at the PX, carrying them around in their pockets and randomly lighting and tossing them as they walked through the beer-infested crowd partying and milling around in the Frankfurt streets. Dean Martin, Winnie's friend, lit one that accidentally slipped out of his hand and into Winnie's jacket pocket, burning a hole right through it, but fizzling out before it reached Winnie's skin. Across the way, the rowdy friends heard a drunk German man hollering something about America GIs. One of the buddies lit a whistler and pitched it toward the German, watching as the burning firework, instead of landing as intended on the sidewalk nearby, fell into the top of the man's boot. The buddies only stuck around long enough to hear the German man yell before he began hopping around, trying to figure out what was searing his leg inside his boot. Even as they felt pity for the man, the Army friends skedaddled in laughter, melting into the reveling crowd.

Winnie was sure he'd gone a bit too far and gotten himself into some deep trouble one day while driving the military bus to deliver the officers' children to a weekend camp. One smart-alecky young boy of about twelve continued to get up and move around the bus, even crossing over the yellow line at the front, despite Winnie's repeatedly stopping the bus and warning him to go back and sit down. "You can't tell me what to do," the boy retorted. "My dad is the Colonel."

Not about to let a twelve-year-old get the best of him, Winnie said to him, "I don't care who your dad is. You go back and sit down. If you get back up one more time, I'm going to give you a whipping."

No sooner were the words out of Winnie's mouth than the boy was up standing in front of the yellow line again. Winnie stopped the bus and took off his Army belt made of canvas webbing, grabbing the buckle and end in his hand leaving a loop hanging. "You aren't gonna hit me," the boy taunted. "My dad is the Colonel. I'll tell my dad."

Winnie grabbed hold of the boy's arm and whacked him once on his bottom with the looped end of the belt. The boy squealed and squalled like he'd been killed, running back to his seat. Winnie delivered the children to the camp and then picked them up again on Sunday, with no further incident. But the next day, Monday morning, Winnie got a telephone call from his First Sergeant with orders that Winnie had to report to Headquarters to the office of the Colonel.

Knowing that he'd gotten himself into a mess this time, Winnie loosened the threads around the stripe on his sleeve so it'd be easier for him to rip it off when the Colonel inevitably ordered him to do so. With dread, Winnie drove out of the casern to the Army Headquarters in downtown Frankfurt. Entering the building, Winnie soon spotted Dave, awaiting his next orders, sitting outside the office door of the Colonel for whom he was the driver. "What the hell have you done now?" Dave wondered, knowing that the only reason Winnie would be at Headquarters is that he must be in big, big trouble. Winnie shook his head as he strode past Dave and down the hallway to another Colonel's office and knocked on the door.

"Specialist Nerich, reporting as ordered," Winnie saluted the Colonel, who looked up unsmiling at Winnie from behind his big wooden desk.

"Did you drive a bus this weekend?" the Colonel asked.

"Yes, Sir," Winnie replied.

"Did you have any problems on the bus?"

Winnie squirmed. "Yes, Sir."

"Explain what happened," demanded the Colonel. And Winnie explained just exactly what had transpired, how after several warnings Winnie had whacked once with his belt the backside of a belligerent boy who refused to obey and threatened to tell his Colonel father. Finishing his story, Winnie took a deep breath and waited for the tongue-lashing that would surely soon follow.

The Colonel stared sternly at Winnie before opening his desk drawer. Pulling out a cigar and holding it out to Winnie, "Here, have a cigar." Confused, but certainly not one to turn down a gift from the Colonel, Winnie accepted. "I've been trying everything to get that boy of mine to behave, but his mother won't let me punish him. I'm glad that someone finally gave him what he deserved."

His meeting with the Colonel was certainly not what Winnie had expected, and he was very grateful for that!

Being in charge of the motor pool and all of its important responsibilities, Winnie was not subject to assignment to many of the extra but necessary duties required of other soldiers. Each morning, Winnie was responsible for two high-priority daily duties: to dispatch the bus to pick up the officers and to dispatch the Colonel's car to go pick up the Colonel. Every dispatch from the motor pool required a trip ticket, a log of every detail involved in every single trip, and keeping the log books accurate and up-to-date was a very important part of Winnie's job.

Soon after a new First Sergeant had been assigned as Winnie's boss, the Sergeant came to Winnie one day and ordered him to be in charge of latrine duty the following morning. "Sergeant, I can't do that," Winnie began to explain.

"Don't tell me you can't do that! I don't want to hear it!" the Sergeant countered. "You are in charge of the latrine, Nerich. That's an order!"

Winnie shrugged his shoulders, realizing he had no choice. That evening, knowing he certainly didn't want to get Dave or himself in trouble with the Colonel, Winnie went ahead and gave Dave his next morning's trip ticket early, but instead of dispatching the bus that picked up the officers as normal, Winnie had to oversee latrine duty as ordered the first thing the following morning.

Latrine duty completed and inspected, Winnie went back to the motor pool about 7:30 a.m. The bus driver, having not yet been dispatched, was worried he would get in trouble and was frantically waiting for Winnie. By this time, the bus should have already picked up the officers and delivered them to Headquarters, but that day the bus was never dispatched because Winnie had been busy following the orders of his First Sergeant. Winnie assured the bus driver that there was nothing for him to worry about; the bus driver was not allowed to drive the bus without his trip ticket. Winnie wasn't to blame either, since he had obeyed a direct order from his First Sergeant. The person to blame, Winnie reasoned, was the new First Sergeant.

Just a few minutes after Winnie arrived at the motor pool that morning, the phone rang. It was First Sergeant, an angry First Sergeant, calling Winnie from the upstairs motor pool office. "Get the jeep ready and pick me up at the bottom of the stairs," he ordered Winnie.

"Where are we going, Sergeant?" Winnie asked, already knowing the answer.

"Headquarters," First Sergeant directed, and Winnie drove out of the casern and the five miles or so to Headquarters downtown. Parking the jeep, the two got out and Winnie followed his Sergeant upstairs to the office of the Sergeant Major, the highest rank of sergeant in the US Army. Everyone knew who the Sergeant Major was, and Winnie had never seen him without a big cigar hanging out of the corner of his mouth.

Hearing the door open, Sergeant Major swiveled his chair around to face his visitors. "Reporting as ordered, Sir," First Sergeant and Winnie greeted their superior with a salute.

The dangling cigar wiggling up and down as he spoke, Sergeant Major demanded, "Why wasn't the officers' bus dispatched this morning?"

Winnie spoke up. "Sergeant Major, First Sergeant gave me a direct order to be in charge of cleaning the latrine, and when I tried to explain why I couldn't, he didn't want to listen. Since I was in charge of latrine detail, I could not go down to motor pool and dispatch the bus."

"First Sergeant, is that true?" Sergeant Major glared as he spoke.

First Sergeant stumbled for words, finally admitted that yes, it was true. At that, Sergeant Major took the long cigar out of his mouth and angrily smashed it straight down into the ashtray on his desk. "From now on, First Sergeant," the words spewing from his mouth, "you are going to clean that shithouse yourself! Leave this man alone, as he has important duties to tend to."

Even though the scolding was justified, Winnie couldn't help but feel just a little sorry for First Sergeant as the Sergeant Major chewed him up one side and down the other. And when his fury subsided and he'd finally run out of steam, Sergeant Major dismissed them. After that incident, First Sergeant wisely left Winnie alone to do his assigned jobs in the motor pool.

Just a short time later, Dave had taken the Colonel to Switzerland and wasn't available to deliver the payroll, so Winnie was assigned to do that important task. Picking up their issued weapons required for payroll delivery duty, Winnie as the driver and a Lieutenant in the passenger seat were both packing pistols, and the clerk in the back was carrying a small carbine. That Saturday morning, after picking up payroll at downtown Headquarters and delivering it to the different companies inside the casern, Winnie and the others went to turn in their guns. Normally on a weekday they would have gone to the Arms Room, but since it was a Saturday the Arms Room was closed, so they instead went to turn their weapons over to First Sergeant to keep in his safe until Monday. The Lieutenant gave his .45 pistol to the clerk and went on his way, leaving Winnie and the clerk to turn in the three guns.

Winnie cleared his weapon and handed it properly to First Sergeant per protocol by holding the barrel with the grip toward First Sergeant. The clerk followed the same procedure, clearing the carbine and handing it over to the officer. But preparing to hand the Lieutenant's pistol over, the clerk carelessly assumed it was empty, and before anyone knew what was happening a bullet shot out of the gun, missing the seated First Sergeant by just a few inches and lodging into the wall behind him.

Not a word was spoken. Realizing that he'd barely missed being struck in the head by a bullet at point-blank range, First Sergeant's face turned pale as a ghost, and Winnie's and the clerk's faces weren't far behind. Deathly silence filled the room, as others along the office hallways clambered quickly toward the gunshot noise to see what had happened.

Needless to say, the clerk wasn't around the base the next day. Handed a carton of cigarettes, as was the custom, that clerk was quickly discharged from duty there and transferred somewhere else, and Winnie never saw him again. Shortly thereafter, that First Sergeant was transferred as well, but the gunshot incident was not forgotten.

One of the most stressful two days of Winnie's 2½ years in Frankfurt followed the Lieutenant's announcement that there would be an inspection of the motor pool by the General, giving Winnie just 48 hours to prepare. "I don't care what you have to do or how you have to do it. Make sure we pass this inspection, Nerich," he was ordered.

With Winnie's motor pool staff consisting of "Me, Myself, and I," Winnie knew he wouldn't be able pull off getting the area inspection-ready in such a short time alone, so he visited the Army jail inside the casern and enlisted the help of ten trustees, non-violent prisoners who were allowed to work under strict supervision. Winnie quickly put them to work, scrubbing, cleaning, and even putting a fresh coat of paint on the walls of the motor pool, and they helped him check the soundness, cleanliness, and reliability of every single vehicle in his fleet. The imprisoned soldiers, glad to get the chance to do something to break the tedium of jail life, worked hard, and a couple of them who had artistic inclinations decided to go even further, creating some artwork to liven up the place. One man painted a colorful mural on the front-facing wall of the grease pit where the workers climbed down to work underneath vehicles, a mural of a monkey hanging out of a tree and holding a grease gun, a depiction of a "grease monkey" that made Winnie smile. Another fellow used his woodworking artistry to create a unique wooden display board of tools to decorate one of the newly-painted motor pool walls.

Two days of hard work later everything was gleaming and looked perfect, and Winnie was ready to show off his motor pool to the General. Meeting the General just outside the motor pool where the shiny vehicles were perfectly lined up, Acting-Sergeant Nerich (at this time he was not actually a sergeant but doing the duties of one while being paid as a SPC4) saluted the General and his accompanying entourage of colonels and other ranked officers. The General walked down the line of vehicles, randomly ordering Winnie to turn the lights on a jeep, start up a bus, check the tire pressure or oil on still another vehicle. Each time Winnie complied, thankful that every order was completed without a single hitch.

As the door to the motor pool opened for him, the General

stepped inside followed by the others, chuckling as the first thing to catch the General's eye was the grease-monkey painting inside the sparkling clean grease pit. He wordlessly walked around the motor pool on the freshly-painted gray floor, bright inside as the newly whitened walls and ceiling reflected the light. Everything was spotless! "Let me see your log book, #14," he ordered, and Winnie obeyed. Paging through that log book before handing it back to Winnie, the General ordered, "Log book #3." Winnie held his breath as the General opened the book and read a few entries before returning it.

"How many people work in the motor pool?" the General questioned Acting-Sergeant Nerich.

"Sir," Winnie answered, "it's Me, Myself, and I."

The General smiled. "Didn't you report to me as Acting-Sergeant Nerich?"

"Yes, Sir."

Turning to the Colonel standing behind him, the General said, "Why is this man not a Sergeant but just an Acting-Sergeant? If he can run the motor pool like this all by himself, he should at least be a Sergeant."

Looking back at Winnie, the General told him, "From now on, you are a Sergeant."

Knowing he'd been given a great compliment but really preferring to become a SP5 instead of a sergeant so he could continue working in his specialty in the motor pool, Winnie spoke up. "Thank you, Sir. But if it's all the same to you, I'd rather be promoted to a SP5 instead."

"As you wish, Nerich," the General nodded, and the men saluted as he began to walk back toward the door, still looking at his immaculate surroundings. Just as he was about to leave, the General turned around. "There is one thing I have to tell you, Nerich. This is not the hospital, this is the motor pool," as his entourage followed him back out into the German sunshine.

Winnie never lived that down, nor did he wish to. The only gig (minor infraction) that Winnie received was that the motor pool was too clean! The Lieutenant was so happy that his company had passed the General's inspection with flying colors, and made sure that everyone was issued passes to go out and celebrate their hard work.

SP5 Nerich from that moment on, Winnie had learned so much in the Army. Thinking back to that October day in 1960 when he'd signed his draft papers in New York City, Winnie knew the last 3½ years had changed him from a boy who had thought he was an adult into a real man, and he was thankful for all the experiences and lessons the Army had taught him.

But the one thing he wanted most still eluded him, and Winnie couldn't get it out of his mind. After being in America for eight years now, he still wasn't an official US citizen.

CHAPTER 25

American Citizen!

1964-1965

Army bases in the United States

"Name the three branches of the government and the responsibilities of each one." Winnie's roommate was sitting on the side of his Army bunk bed, quizzing him on the thick manual that Winnie had been studying for months now.

Answering confidently, that question was an easy one for Winnie. For a man who could barely read English, studying for the citizenship test was extra-challenging. Thankfully, Winnie's memory was remarkable, and once he learned a fact it was in his head to stay. He couldn't help but wonder how many natural-born American citizens would know even half of what he'd memorized, and Winnie found out later that very few did.

The whole journey to citizenship had been a long, drawn-out exercise in frustration. Winnie had tried his best to avoid taking the exam (and the necessary long hours of studying for it!) by requesting twice to be sent to Vietnam or Korea. Had the Army granted his request, per protocol Winnie would have automatically been granted citizenship immediately. But, as the Army clerk told Winnie when his latest request had been denied, the paperwork required to do that was too much trouble for the Army; it was much easier to send an unwilling young man who was already a citizen into a war zone than to send a willing green-card immigrant. If there's one thing Winnie had learned during his time in the military, it was that the Army didn't always make much sense.

And so he'd studied. With the help of his roommates, Winnie had pored over the thick citizenship manual until it was ragged and dirty. After receiving his green card in August of 1960, Winnie was told he had to wait three years before being considered for citizenship. As soon as he was eligible, Winnie had applied and was, in fact, on his way to New York City for the necessary testing when his airplane flying from Germany was diverted to Scotland due to mechanical problems. A higher-ranking officer took the last seat on the next plane out, sending the disappointed young soldier Winnie back to Germany. Winnie contacted the Red Cross to find out how he should proceed, and was told to wait until he was stateside again to trade in his green card status for true citizenship. Wait, again. He had no other choice.

Meanwhile, big changes were ahead for Winnie. The Army had given him orders to go back stateside in May of 1964. Dave left for the US two months ahead of Winnie, a sad day for the two close buddies as they bid each other good-bye with promises to meet up again someday. But truthfully Winnie wondered if they would ever see each other again. So many great memories of fun times during their years in Germany, Dave was the closest friend Winnie had ever known. But those days were behind them now; it was time for both men to move forward with their own lives.

Leaving Germany in early May of 1964, Winnie headed back to New York City to spend his 30-day leave with his cousin Nick. He'd left his new car, a gray 1964 Volkswagen station wagon with "US Government" license plates, to be shipped home free of charge on the next available military ship. The timing was fortunate for Winnie, as the Army only shipped personal cars home for its soldiers four times a year, and the ship and Winnie's plane left Germany at about the same time. With any luck, Winnie wouldn't have too long of a wait to get his car back home in America.

A couple of weeks into his leave, Winnie received word from the Army that his car was available for pick-up at a port in New Jersey. Arriving at the port, Winnie was shocked to see someone he knew. Dave was also there to pick up his car! The two friends hugged and laughed, amazed at the coincidental timing and chance meeting. Dave told Winnie that he'd come to New Jersey from his home in Indiana to pick up his car, and invited Winnie to come home with him over the long Memorial Day weekend.

Still enjoying his leave from the Army, Winnie had nothing better to do, and he was glad to follow his friend Dave back to Indiana for a few days. He'd heard so much about Dave's family; now he was going to finally meet them in person. Dave followed Winnie as he drove back to Nick's to pick up his belongings, meeting Winnie's cousin for the first time, and Dave's car led the way out of New York City with Winnie's Volkswagen right behind, heading south and west to Dave's home state of Indiana.

The interstate highway system was being built at that time, so Dave and Winnie followed the new Interstate 70 as much as possible, getting off to drive on US 40 for the sections that were still not complete. Just barely across the Indiana state line from Ohio, Dave followed the orange signs off the under-construction interstate and onto Indiana's State Road 38. Being in a different part of the country that he hadn't before seen, Winnie watched the fields roll past his windows as he followed Dave west on 38 through the tiny town of Greens Fork, Indiana. What a funny name for a town, Winnie thought!

A few miles down the road, the two cars approaching the small town of Hagerstown, as they rounded a curve a charming stone house and garage caught Winnie's eye. "Someday I'm going to own a nice little place like that, my very own garage and house," Winnie thought as he drove past the little stone structure.

Dave's hometown was New Castle, Indiana, just a dozen or so more miles away. Arriving at his family's home in town, Dave introduced Winnie to his dad, his step-mom, and his three brothers, who all gave Winnie a hearty, friendly welcome.

"What are your plans for Memorial Day weekend?" Winnie asked Dave, knowing that this holiday marked the unofficial beginning of summer in the United States.

"We're going to Kentucky!" Dave responded excitedly.

Winnie wondered, "Why Kentucky?"

"Because," Dave said, "everybody in New Castle goes to Kentucky for Memorial Day."

Not one to question the traditions of Dave and his New Castle kin, Winnie joined Dave and his brothers Lee, Warren, and Ray, the five of them piling into the two cars and heading south to visit relatives in Monticello, Kentucky.

Knowing that alcohol would surely liven up the holiday weekend, Winnie offered to buy some to share with his hosts. Asking Dave's cousin where he should go to get some, the cousin informed Winnie that they lived in a dry county and he wouldn't be able to purchase any alcohol locally. But the state of Tennessee was only twelve miles away, so Winnie and Dave hopped into Winnie's Volkswagen and bought a couple of cases of beer just on the other side of the state line.

The men enjoyed the beer that night, but it didn't take long to go through two cases, so the next afternoon Winnie suggested they needed something else a little stronger, maybe some moonshine. The young men looked at Dave's cousin as he spoke, pointing down the gravel road. "Go down the road about two miles. When you come to the big black mailbox, make a left and drive up that long lane. The first house you come to on the right hand side, stop and blow your horn three times. Those guys will sell you whatever you want."

Dave was busy talking, so Winnie volunteered. "I'm going to run down there and get some," he said, jumping in his Volkswagen and creating a roll of dust as the car disappeared down the country road.

Finding the place easily, Winnie stopped in front of the house, blew his horn three times, and waited. After a few moments, a gray-haired gentleman using a cane slowly walked down to Winnie's car, and Winnie stepped out onto the gravel driveway to meet him.

"May I help you?" asked the wrinkled old man.

"Yes, sir," Winnie answered. "I'd like to buy a case of beer and a quart of moonshine."

The old fellow stared Winnie straight in the eye, shaking his head. "Oh, no. My son lives here and we are Christian people. We don't believe in drinking."

Winnie was confused and embarrassed. "I'm so sorry, sir. I was told I could buy liquor here. I apologize for bothering you." The old man nodded, and Winnie climbed into his car and drove back to where Dave's family was waiting.

"Did you get it?" Dave's cousin walked toward the car.

"No," Winnie answered. "I went to the house you told me to, but the old man who lived there said they were Christian people and didn't believe in drinking."

Dave's cousin paused for a moment, then began howling in laughter. "Damn," he managed to get out between fits of amusement. "Talking like you do, driving a car like no one in these parts has ever seen before with a license plate that says 'US Government', he thought you were a revenuer! You wouldn't even be able to get a glass of water, let alone moonshine!" And the others joined him in a good chuckle over the incident.

"I'll go with you," Dave's cousin said, getting into the passenger seat, and this time the old man at the house down the road smiled and happily obliged his neighbor's request, selling the two illegal moonshine.

After a great Memorial Day weekend, Dave and company drove back home to New Castle on Monday. His 30-day leave nearly over, Winnie still had 16 months left on his Army enlistment, and he reported for duty as ordered to Fort Polk, Louisiana in early June 1964.

Finding out the military installation at Fort Polk had no jobs for Winnie's specialty, Winnie and the officers wondered why he had been sent there at all. But after a few days, Winnie was reassigned to the huge Army base at Fort Benning, Georgia.

It was quickly apparent that Winnie wasn't needed at Fort Benning either. Reporting for duty as ordered at the base motor pool, Winnie unpacked and settled into his assigned bunk. The next morning, excited to start his new Army job, Winnie was surprised to learn there were five mechanics in the motor pool. Five! He'd been the only mechanic all those months in Germany. Not only were there five mechanics, there were also six sergeants, and not nearly enough work to keep all of them busy.

"What do you want me to do?" Winnie inquired of the main sergeant in charge of the motor pool.

"Look busy," was his reply.

Winnie looked around for a few minutes, picked up a broom and began to sweep the floor. The sergeant rushed over to him. "Oh no, Nerich. You can't do that. You're a SP5, you can't sweep the floor!"

"Then what can I do?" Winnie asked. This was crazy! Used to having more work than time, Winnie was not one to sit still, and he needed a job.

"Look busy," the sergeant repeated.

So that's what Winnie did, the best he could. He'd dispatch a jeep to himself and go to the PX, run errands for anyone he could find, picking up people at the train station, anything and everything Winnie could think of to keep himself from being bored out of his mind.

Although his time in Georgia did not seem very productive from the Army standpoint, one wonderful thing happened during Winnie's two-month stay there. With extra time on his hands to study, Winnie finally had a chance to make his citizenship dream come true. The waiting game was finally over, and on the designated day, Winnie, proudly wearing his US Army uniform, drove to the courthouse in Columbus, Georgia to take the citizenship test.

As Winnie awaited his turn with the other citizenship candidates, he wasn't sure what to expect. His English reading skills were still not very good, so he was glad to find out the test would be oral. One by one, the line slowly moved as candidates in front of him were tested. Right in front of Winnie was a young woman with a baby in her arms. He overheard the tester ask her, "Who did this country belong to before it became the United States?"

When the young woman replied, "The Indians," she was congratulated on passing her test and sent on her way. Winnie couldn't believe how easy that was! And all this time, he'd been sweating and studying. This citizenship test was going to be a piece of cake.

He shouldn't have celebrated quite so soon. As he stepped forward, the man asking the test questions grilled him mercilessly.

What is the President's job? The Vice-President's job? How many Senators? How many Congressmen? How many stars and stripes on the flag, and what do they represent? How many judges are on the Supreme Court? What is the chain of command in the US Army? On which side of a public speaker should the American flag be displayed? Which direction do you face if you are saying the "Pledge of Allegiance" without a flag in sight?

On and on and on, 26 questions in all, each time Winnie responding as best he could recall. He was even asked a couple of random questions about the Georgia state government that were not in his study book. Winnie was grateful he'd followed his hunch, stopping at a local pawn shop on his way in and asking the proprietor the name of the mayor of Columbus, Georgia as well as another question about the local government. As it turned out, both of those questions were part of the 26-item grilling, and had Winnie not stopped and asked at the pawn shop, he'd have surely missed those two questions.

Despite his nervousness, Winnie passed with flying colors, only missing one question: he answered that there were twelve judges on the Supreme Court, when in fact there are twelve JURORS but only nine JUDGES. (A fact, he doubted, that few natural-born citizens knew.) He was astonished at how detailed and difficult the test was, and later, after being sworn in along with his class of 74 brand new citizens of the United States of America, Winnie found the tester and asked the question that nagged at him.

"Why did you ask me 26 difficult questions when the lady in front of me was asked only one very easy question?" Winnie wondered.

The man looked Winnie in the eyes as he answered. "Because you are wearing the Army uniform, because you are fighting for me and my country, I wanted to be sure you knew what you were doing and understood the country you are fighting for."

A few weeks later, Winnie received in his Army mail the precious papers for which he'd waited so long and worked so hard. He was an American citizen! But as Winnie was happily examining the certificate, he noticed that his last name was misspelled on the official document. "Nirich," it said, not "Nerich."

The misspelling took Winnie off-guard for a moment, but he quickly decided what he would do. Nothing. Not about to jeopardize the citizenship status that he'd dreamed about for so long, from here on out, Winnie decided, his name would be Vincent Nirich. Njiric — Nerich — Nirich… what did it matter? He was a US citizen now, that's all that mattered.

His Army time at Fort Benning was boring with not enough to keep Winnie working. The hours crept by and Winnie quickly tired of inventing his own busy work. He finally went to the Company Sergeant and asked to be transferred to someplace where his skills could be used.

Aberdeen Proving Grounds, Maryland… as a mechanics instructor? Winnie had trouble picturing himself as an instructor, but at least he'd be busy. So to Aberdeen he went, working as an instructor in the shop area, teaching young soldiers how to change tires, fix problems, change oil, replace parts, and keep the military vehicles road-ready. He'd been reluctant at first, but Winnie liked sharing his knowledge with new mechanics and came to enjoy his time as the shop instructor.

But after a few weeks, Winnie was switched from being a shop instructor to teaching the classroom portion, which was not as good of a fit. Several times Winnie was reprimanded for using the wrong names for parts of a vehicle…Winnie called one part a "drive shaft" when the proper Army term was "propeller shaft"; Winnie's name for the vehicle's "rear end" should be correctly called the "rear differential." His superiors also didn't appreciate Winnie's joke-telling to keep the soldiers' attention, and he wasn't allowed to give them breaks or let them out of class early, and after a while Winnie even shared his frustration with the Colonel who didn't appreciate Winnie's opinion on the matter.

Another source of frustration, but sometimes amusement as well, were the officers who had just graduated from college and were assigned to oversee Winnie. The young lieutenants were undoubtedly book-smart, but they had no knowledge of vehicles at all. But that didn't stop them from questioning Winnie about his teaching. One young officer demanded why Winnie wasn't teaching the students how to grease and properly maintain "muffler bearings." Apparently someone had set the young man up for embarrassment, since there were no such parts as muffler bearings. The green lieutenant began chewing Winnie out for omitting such a crucial part of vehicle maintenance, even though Winnie tried repeatedly to explain that there is no such part. Frustrated, the young officer talked to the sergeant in charge about Winnie's refusal to listen, and finally realized his leg had been pulled when the sergeant began laughing and explained that there are no such things as muffler bearings. It wasn't the last incident for the gullible young lieutenant, as the mechanics had him believing that windshield wiper blades needed to be sharpened regularly and that left-handers used specially-designed monkey wrenches.

Winnie quickly tired of all the daily shenanigans. So even though the Army recruiters tried to entice him to re-enlist for three more years with the promise of being promoted to an E-6 Specialist, Winnie decided he was done with the Army, and in October 1965 Winnie traded his military life for a new start as a civilian US citizen.

CHAPTER 26

Living the Dream

1966

New Castle, Indiana

Walking east down Broad Street in New Castle, Indiana, Winnie and Ray were willing to take any job they could find, but so far the two had come up empty-handed. Every store, bank, bar, used car lot, filling station, and every other business establishment told them the same thing as they'd heard at the county unemployment office earlier that day… there were no job openings.

Leaving the Army in October 1965, Winnie stayed in Maryland for a couple of months, working at the Goodyear store there. Finally having his passport in hand, Winnie flew back to Europe to visit his family for the first time since he'd left over thirteen years before. He surprised his family and spent a joyous Christmas holiday with them before coming back to the US to start his new life as a civilian.

Having had his fill of New York City, and since Dave's family had become like a second family to him, Dave's hometown of New Castle seemed like the logical place for a fresh start. Soon after getting home from his own stint in the Army, Dave had married and the newlyweds were living in the next county over in Anderson,

Indiana. But Dave's father and step-mother graciously opened their small New Castle home to Dave's Army friend, Winnie sleeping in his car and sharing the Catron family's kitchen and bathroom facilities.

Of the four Catron brothers, Ray was the only one unmarried and still living with his father and step-mother. Having just been laid off, he and Winnie were in the same boat, so they began pounding the pavement side by side, looking for work. Unable to draw any unemployment money until 30 days following his Army discharge, with a car payment and insurance due as well as living expenses to cover, Winnie was desperate for any kind of paying job.

And so, beginning at 12th and Broad Streets in downtown New Castle, Winnie and Ray walked for blocks and blocks with no success. It seemed there were no job opportunities available in New Castle.

About to give up and wondering what their next step might be, Winnie expected the same response when he and Ray walked into the small gas station at 27th and Broad. "Do you need any help?" Winnie asked the owner.

"No," he answered half-heartedly. "But I'd sure like to sell you this place."

Winnie, surprised, laughed as he responded. "What with? $13.50? That's all I have."

Looking squarely at Winnie, the man said, "Are you really interested in buying it?"

"For $13.50?" Winnie countered, not quite sure what to make of this strange conversation.

"Okay," the man said.

Winnie turned to Ray. "Is this crazy, Ray?" Ray encouraged him to listen, and they did as the man explained how they might come to a deal. Getting in his car, they drove down to the bulk fuel plant that supplied the gas station to talk with the plant managers.

"I'm asking $2400 for the station and everything in it," the gas station owner told Winnie and Ray, as the bulk plant owner, who had introduced himself as Dale Copeland, listened.

"I don't have any money," Winnie countered.

"That's no problem," Mr. Copeland jumped in. "We will pay the owner the $2400 for the station, fill your tanks with gasoline, and give you everything you need to get started. Then as you make money, you can pay us back."

Winnie looked back at Ray, who'd been standing silently at his side all this time. "Ray, what do we have to lose?"

Ray quickly answered, "$13.50."

Thinking for a moment, Winnie agreed. Then turning to the three men, he said, "I'll play your silly game. Okay, we'll buy the gas station." Pausing, he remembered one small detail. "We don't even have enough money to operate a cash register."

So Mr. Copeland quickly loaned Winnie $50 right then and there, and after a round of handshakes, Winnie and Ray found themselves partners and co-owners of what they soon named the R&W Sinclair station and garage.

All the paperwork was signed the next morning, Winnie and Ray immediately taking reigns of the business, and just like that Winnie was an American business owner. Not able to pay the mechanic who worked there anything other than commission, the mechanic left and it was just the two of them, Winnie and Ray, who ran the shop and garage. Winnie set up an old Army cot in the back room of the station, and that's where he slept until he made enough money to rent a small house a few months later.

While most stations were selling gas for about 25-cents per gallon, Winnie and Ray ran a Grand Opening special of 17-cents for a gallon of gas, gaining new customers to join the station's established ones. Besides pumping gasoline, they also did minor repairs and car maintenance in the garage, and slowly but surely Winnie and Ray began to get ahead, making enough profit each month to pay their lenders and still have a little left over for themselves.

Winnie did learn a hard lesson about how running American businesses worked. Coming from a Communist country, Winnie thought the sales taxes he collected from his customers was his to keep, a token from the government for servicing the public. So he'd been keeping that money, and when the amount reached about $1300, tax agents eventually caught up with him and threatened to throw him into jail if he didn't pay those taxes. Winnie managed to scrape together the money needed, avoiding imprisonment and learning a very valuable lesson the hard way.

Soon Winnie and Ray were able to hire a mechanic, then two, and over the next few years Winnie would hire and mentor many young mechanics. When he got a little money ahead, Winnie bought a race car, and spent many Sunday evenings at the local racetrack cheering on his driver. After several months, Ray decided to move to Wisconsin and sold his half of the business to Winnie for $1000. By this time the garage was paid off, and Winnie managed to scrape together the thousand dollars, becoming sole owner and operator of his newly renamed business, Winnie's Sinclair. The pieces of his American dream were all falling into place.

Only one piece was missing, and it was a big one. All he needed to complete his American dream was a wife and family. But Winnie didn't realize it yet.

CHAPTER 27

At Home in Indiana

1967

Hagerstown, Indiana

Winnie wasn't really looking for a woman with whom to spend the rest of his life. At just 29 years old, there was plenty of time for that. He was in love with his race car and enthralled with his business; life was great, just as it was. Since owning the garage, Winnie had dated a few different girls, but no one quite struck his fancy, and he was surely being a little extra-cautious, not wanting to jump into a marriage and commitment for which he wasn't yet ready. He'd made that mistake once, and Winnie was smart enough not to repeat it.

So when the wife of Winnie's employee wanted to fix Winnie up with one of her girlfriends, Winnie didn't get too excited. In fact, he never even bothered to show up for what was supposed to be their first date. A couple of weeks later, the tenacious matchmaker arranged for another meeting of the two, but this time Julie was the one who didn't show. Winnie had met his match, and he had to admit he was a little intrigued.

One Sunday afternoon in June 1967, a friend of Winnie's named Carl stopped by the station accompanied by a teenage boy.

"Come on, Winnie. This boy will close up the station. You're coming with me," he said.

"I can't go," Winnie protested. "I need to stay here until closing time."

But Winnie finally gave in to his friend's insistence, reluctantly leaving his garage keys in the hands of the young boy and hopping into the car beside his friend. They were going to the races, Carl told Winnie.

Planning to go later anyway since his car was racing, Winnie didn't quite understand yet what the rush was all about. When Carl drove the car to his house, Winnie finally began to figure out what was going on when he was introduced to a pretty young woman named Julie. Winnie had to admit Julie was cute and very nice, her sparkling eyes and bright smile charming him, but he was a little perturbed at being tricked into yet another date that he wasn't so sure he wanted.

Arriving at Mt. Lawn Speedway outside of New Castle, Julie sat with the other couple up in the bleachers, but Winnie went down to the pits. With his car racing that night, Winnie had no intention of sitting way up in the bleachers away from the action when he knew he'd have a lot more fun with his car's crew in the pits. Not wanting to be completely rude to his unsolicited "date," Winnie grabbed himself a hot dog and drink during intermission and climbed up into the bleachers to join his friends for a few minutes.

As Winnie took a big bite from his hot dog, Carl looked at him. "Where is Julie's hot dog and pop?" he asked Winnie. Shrugging his shoulders, Winnie pointed toward the concession stand and Carl, a little irritated that this arranged date wasn't going as planned, went down and bought Julie's supper himself.

When the four of them got back to Carl's house later that night, Winnie discovered that Julie was driving a small Ford car with a loud exhaust system. Julie was a sweet girl, and Winnie liked her and knew he could help with her car. It had just so happened that just three days before, Winnie's mechanic had put a brand new exhaust system in a car very similar to Julie's, and as the mechanic was turning back in to the station after road-testing the repaired car early that morning, another car had broadsided him and totaled the car.

Hearing the noisy muffler on Julie's car, Winnie told her, "I've got a crashed car just like yours sitting behind my garage, with a brand new exhaust system. If you want, bring your car in and I'll put that new exhaust system on your car."

Julie replied, "Thanks, but I don't have any money for that." She hadn't decided yet if she liked Winnie or not. He was okay, she guessed, but it didn't take a genius to realize he wasn't looking for a relationship. Julie had already been burned pretty badly in the love department herself, and she certainly wasn't eager to repeat her mistakes either.

"Aw, don't worry about the money," Winnie told her. "I'll be glad to do it, no charge. Just bring it down."

Winnie fixed Julie's car as promised, just two days before the 4th of July, 1967. And try as he might, all the while he was working on her car Winnie just couldn't get Julie out of his mind. So when she came to pick it up, he casually asked her, "What are you doing for the 4th of July?"

"Oh, nothing special. I'll probably take the kids to see the fireworks," Julie answered.

Julie was a single mother, raising seven-year-old Gary and four-year-old Angie by herself, divorced from their father for a couple of years. Winnie already knew about the children; Julie was clearly proud of her beautiful babies. Loving children himself, that didn't bother Winnie a bit and in fact added to his attraction to Julie.

"Would you mind if I picked you and the kids up and took

you to the fireworks?" Winnie asked her. Julie paused briefly before accepting, telling him where she lived, and two days later Winnie drove his 1959 Oldsmobile convertible into her country driveway and knocked on her door.

The most adorable little girl with a headful of ringlets and curls was standing by the kitchen table as Julie opened the door. "This is Angie," she said, as Winnie bent over to greet the child. "And this is Gary," as Angie's older brother stood next to his mother. The children and Winnie immediately liked each other, and Gary thought he was riding on top of the world in the convertible to the fireworks show in nearby small Hagerstown.

What a great time the four of them had! Winnie bought the children some candy and drinks, and they sat together in Winnie's convertible under the stars watching the fireworks. Julie loved how Winnie treated her children, and that night was the beginning of their love relationship that would last them both the rest of their lives.

Neither of them were ready to jump back into marriage again at first, but over time they both knew that's exactly what they wanted. Winnie remembered the advice of his father Ilija, repeated so many years ago back in Yugoslavia. "Never marry a woman until you have known her for all four seasons."

And so, over the next year, Winnie dated Julie and helped finish building the addition onto her house. Before he could get married again, Winnie had some loose legal ends to tie up, as although he'd been single for a long time, he'd never legally divorced. Winnie's lawyer tried in vain for several months to locate Margaret, but when all avenues had been exhausted and she could not be found, Winnie was finally granted a divorce by the courts. He also worked through his new Catholic priest to have his first marriage annulled by the church and finally, after several months, Julie and Winnie were both legally free to marry.

One day when Winnie came by Julie's house to see her, after

giving her a quick kiss, he wanted to speak with Angie and Gary in the bedroom. Closing the door behind them, Julie wondered what was going on, as behind that door Winnie asked the children if it would be all right with them if he married their mother. Gary and Angie were delighted that Winnie would be their new father, and Julie's heart melted knowing that Winnie cared enough about her children to even ask.

On April 5, 1968, nine months (that covered the four seasons!) after their first real date at the fireworks show, Winnie and Julie were married in the White Branch Church of the Brethren, the tiny country church where Julie and her family had attended church her whole life. For their honeymoon trip, Winnie and Julie went to Columbus, Ohio for Sinclair school, where Julie learned how to do books for the gas station and Winnie learned about customer service and other business issues... perhaps not the most romantic of honeymoons, but it was all paid for by the Sinclair Oil Corporation. They settled into Julie's home, and a little later Winnie took Julie on another trip, this time to New York City to meet his cousin Nick and family.

Ready to start a business in Hagerstown, soon after they married Winnie began looking to sell his New Castle garage and buy something nearby. His opportunity came when Winnie discovered a charming little stone garage and house for sale on the east edge of Hagerstown.

It was the very same stone garage and house that Winnie had noticed on his very first trip to Indiana, driving through Hagerstown on his way to Dave's hometown of New Castle! Smiling to himself, Winnie recalled that day, how after all the miles he'd driven it had been that very property that had caught his eye and made him wish he might buy a place just like that someday. Now here he was, a few years later, with a chance to make yet another of his dreams a reality.

So Winnie paid a visit to a realtor in town, Woody Bowman, who had listed the property. The two men didn't know each other at all, but Woody knew Julie's family very well, all of them attending the same church and Julie being one of his daughter Karen's best friends. Woody had a good feeling about this ambitious young man Julie had married, and he was willing to help him if he could. Woody took Winnie to the property and they looked around, but Winnie's heart fell when Woody told him that the owner wanted $14,000 in cash for the property.

$14,000?! Winnie couldn't wrap his mind around such a price! Dave had offered to buy Winnie's Sinclair for $2000, but by the time he paid all the bank and legal fees Winnie figured he'd probably have just about $1000 left over, a drop in the financial bucket compared to what this property's owner was asking.

"I don't have that kind of money," Winnie told Woody.

"How much do you have?" Woody asked.

"Only about $1000. There's no way I can even get a loan for that amount, so I guess buying it is out of the question unless the owner is willing to sell it to me on contract."

Woody replied, "No, she's not willing to do that."

Then Winnie, half-joking, said to the realtor, "Why don't YOU buy it from her and then YOU can sell it to me on contract?"

Woody paused for a moment, thinking. "I don't know if I can do that. Let me talk to my wife."

A glimmer of hope flashed through Winnie's mind. It was a long shot, but maybe, just maybe...

Woody called Winnie a couple of days later. He'd managed to convince an area bank to loan $7000 toward the property. Woody and his wife Maedoris were willing to front the rest of the money, and Winnie could pay them back as he got the money to do so. Agreeing to pay Woody an extra $1000 for his help along with interest for the property, Winnie and Julie signed a contract with Woody and purchased the stone property at the edge of Hagerstown that Winnie had first set his mind on several years before, a garage and a small restaurant business.

A year after they were married, Winnie legally adopted Julie's children Gary and Angie. Then in April of 1970, Winnie and Julie welcomed the birth of their son, naming him Vincent Nirich, Junior.

Over the years Winnie added a used car business to his garage and restaurant, making many, many friends and business contacts along the way. But he never forgot the kindness and generosity, the confidence shown him by three men who believed in the young man and helped him achieve his dream: Dale Copeland who owned the bulk gas company and had helped him and Ray get R&W Sinclair started, Woody Bowman who helped him finance his Hagerstown business, and Tuffy Davis who became his good friend and business partner buying and selling used cars.

Even though miles of ocean separate them, Winnie stays connected with his brother and sisters back home. After his father Ilija died, Winnie, as the Njiric heir, signed over his legal rights to the Croatian property to his brother Ivo, who continues to maintain the family home as a boarding house for tourists visiting the magnificent Adriatic Sea area. Winnie goes back as often as he is able, sharing the home of his childhood with Julie, his three children, and his adult grandson.

God has blessed Winnie/Vinnie/Visko his entire life, and Winnie knows that if God hadn't been watching over him every step of his incredible journey, it is doubtful he would even be alive much less enjoy the life he has today. From the day he took his first breath in a wooden rowboat on the waters of the Adriatic Sea, even though he's made his home among the cornfields of Indiana, Winnie's heart will always be inexplicably tied to the sea. It's been a remarkable journey, but Winnie never gave up, and through the grace of God Winnie made little Visko's dream come true.

Because, if Visko Ivo Njiric was anything, he was unsinkable.

Epilogue

December 1965

Stikovica, Yugoslavia

Franica was tired. Exhausted, really. For days and days she'd been working even harder than usual, trying to get ready for Christmas.

Christmas was her favorite holiday, but it was exhausting. Both physically and emotionally exhausting. Christmas was a family time, with so many, many memories playing through her mind as Franica decorated her home and cooked and baked those special recipes that her family only enjoyed at Christmas.

Most were happy memories, but Christmas always unleashed a lingering sadness that Franica tried to keep in check the rest of the year. It had been thirteen years since she'd seen her firstborn son, Visko. Oh yes, after the absolute worst year of her life thinking he had perished at sea, how joyful had been her tears when she found out he was alive and well in New York City. Not only was she unbelievably relieved that her son was not dead, Franica was also very proud of Visko and so happy for him. Countless times he'd shared with his mother his dream of living in the United States of America, and Franica was thrilled for Visko that he'd made those childhood dreams come true.

Visko was 27 now, Franica thought. The last time she'd seen her son he was a teenager of 14, so even though she knew her baby was now a man, in Franica's mind and heart Visko was still her little boy.

Cleaning her kitchen after a long day of baking, Franica smiled remembering the time Visko had tried to sneak some Christmas cake so long ago. While she couldn't blame her husband for being angry that day when the cake collapsed under his knife, Franica felt Ilija had been a bit too harsh on the boy. After all, it had been Christmas Day, and he was just a mischievous boy. But, as she had so many times before, that morning Franica had held her tongue as Ilija punished Visko.

Older now and much wiser, Franica wished she had spoken up more in Visko's defense. Too often she had been silent while Visko received sometimes unwarranted punishment from Ilija and Grandma Njiric. He was a good boy deep down, Franica knew. Franica believed she understood her son more intimately than anyone, and she admired him more than she had ever shared.

How she longed to see him! Franica knew she would never travel to America, and she wondered when and if Visko would ever return home again. Thirteen Christmases had come and gone, and with each one Franica's hopes of ever seeing Visko grew ever dimmer.

But that didn't keep Franica from dreaming and hoping, as she wondered what his life was like in America. Occasionally she'd get a letter from Visko, which she read and re-read until the paper was dirty and the ink smeared, then she'd put it away in a safe place before the writing became completely illegible. Franica loved all five of her children, for sure, but being her firstborn and all they had suffered through together during the war, Visko held a special place in Franica's heart.

Epilogue

Nostalgia washed over Franica as she made her final swipe with the dishcloth across the table. She was ready for bed...enough memories for tonight.

Turning out the kitchen light, she heard a car pull up outside the house. Peering through the kitchen curtains into the darkness, Franica with the help of the dim lights outside could vaguely see the outline of a car, one she didn't recognize.

"Who in the world could it be," she thought, "driving here at 9:00 at night?" And she bid her adult daughter Cicilija to see what the stranger wanted.

As Cicilija opened the front gates, Franica pulled her woolen shawl more tightly around her tired body against the chilly December ocean breeze and stepped onto the upper terrace outside the kitchen. Taking a deep breath of the familiar salty air, Franica gazed out across the sea that she loved so much. She never tired of this view from the terrace, high above the sparkling waters of the Adriatic. Every time she looked across those waters, she imagined her Visko on the other side of the vast ocean. Perhaps that's why she loved the sea so much...it reminded her of her Visko.

Franica's heart seized as she heard the man's voice. Speaking in German, the man asked Cicilija, "Do you have any rooms for rent?"

Suddenly the seashore was spinning around her, as the voice, HIS VOICE, drifted upward. Although she'd never heard him speak German before, that voice had spoken to her thousands of times in her dreams, and Franica was smiling as her world became dark and she slumped to the cement terrace floor.

Hearing the thump of her mother falling on the terrace above, Cicilija rushed up the stairs with the man close behind her. As they both knelt, Franica groggily began to rouse from her faint. Was she dreaming? For as she opened her eyes, she looked into what was unmistakably the blue eyes of her Visko.

He spoke again, and Franica realized at once that she wasn't dreaming at all. Visko was home!!!

Why had she even doubted? Of course he would come home, at least for a little while. And that, for now, was more than enough for Franica.

She'd known it all along, from the frantic day she'd given birth to him through all the harrowing circumstances he'd survived in his young life. Franica knew without a doubt that if her Visko was anything, he was unsinkable.

photo from Winnie Nirich collection

Franica and Ilija Njiric, early 1970s

Notes from the Author

July 31, 2014

I've come to the conclusion that there are two kinds of people in this world... the survivors and the giver-uppers. When the going gets tough and the future looks impossible, there are those who fight and scrap with every cell of their beings, and there are those who may battle half-heartedly for a short while but quickly throw in the towel to irreversible despair or even death.

Winnie is a survivor. How he is even alive today to share it with us is amazing... God certainly had extraordinary plans for him from his very humble beginning!

I was a ten years old when Winnie entered my life. My first memories of him were at our extended family's Christmas celebration in 1967. Of course, I had heard tales of this wild, fun Yugoslavian man who was dating Dad's cousin Judy (whom Winnie calls "Julie"), but that Christmas Eve is the first time we all met him. All of us cousins were crazy over him, and we still are.

So it is with deepest gratitude that I am privileged to write down his story. Authoring a book has never been even remotely on my radar, but I guess I've learned to never say "never"!

And so our journey together begins... my journey as an author and Winnie's journey as the story-teller. Something tells me this is going to be an adventure... I've come to expect nothing less when Winnie is involved!

August 14, 2014   In Winnie's Home, Rural Indiana

Sitting across from Winnie at his homey country kitchen table, I continue to be amazed at this remarkable man and his incredible story. Really, even in my wildest imaginings I couldn't have made up a story as extraordinary as the one I've been listening to him tell me the past couple of Thursdays.

Now 76 years old, despite his graying hair, Winnie still has a boyish look about him, his blue eyes still sparkling as they must have in the face of young Visko so many decades and indeed lifetimes ago, in what must have been another world and another time. Even though she's heard his stories many, many times in their long 46-year marriage, Winnie's wife Judy (my dad's first cousin) still is amazed at his resiliency and the horrors he lived in his early years. She and I shake our heads in disbelief, wondering how in the world he ever survived and landed here in this kitchen in the middle of cornfields in Indiana.

photo by Terry Gray

As he speaks, Winnie fingers the worn gold band on his ring finger, the same wedding ring his Grandma Amilija Njiric was given during her 1909 ceremony when she wed Grandpa Visko Njiric. He slipped it off this afternoon to show me the inscription inside, her initials "A.N." and the year "1909." No doubt, this was a wealthy man's gift to his young bride as most Stikovica villagers would not have had the means to buy a wedding ring. If only that ring could talk...

August 21, 2014

I don't drink alcohol, never have. But today Winnie wanted me to take a swig of Croatian moonshine. How could I refuse? I mean, it's all in the name of research. WOW... it made my toes curl!

September 12, 2014

I am so thankful to be sitting here today across from Winnie. What an emotional roller-coaster of a week this has been!

Most Thursdays I drop off a couple of newly-written chapters to Judy in the morning for Winnie and her to read at lunchtime while I spend the morning visiting my Mama and Dad, Lois and Bud House, who live just a few miles away. Then when I arrive to interview Winnie later in the afternoon, he helps me correct anything that I've written that is not quite right. It is HIS story, not mine, and I want it to be as accurate as his memory allows.

But this is Friday, and honestly I didn't even know if I would be sitting here today or ever again. Winnie gave us all a big scare, spending all week in the hospital, and just two days ago a pacemaker was implanted into his chest. Last night he came home and today he insisted that we continue with the book. So I hadn't had a chance to give them the fresh chapters to read ahead of time. Winnie and Judy wanted me to read it to them this week, so I began. Why was I feeling so shaky and nervous as I began to read? Because deep inside I really, REALLY want them both to be pleased with this book, I want to live up to what my mind has imagined to be their expectations.

So I read, pausing occasionally to clarify a thought or to ask Winnie for input. But mostly, the kitchen was pin-drop quiet except for my voice. Every few paragraphs I looked up at Winnie to see his reaction. And what I saw astonished me. His face was pale and tired, his arm in a sling to give the pacemaker incision time to heal. This week has taken a toll on him. But his eyes, those blue eyes, were listening intently to me and he was smiling, and I could almost see his mind remembering the scenes from 65 years ago that my words were describing. He was happy, and yes, I'm pretty sure he is pleased.

September 18, 2014

Vincie joined us today. Vincent Nirich, Jr., the son of Winnie and Judy. Vincie (I still call him by his childhood nickname even though now he is very much a man!) is creating the cover for the book, and we met in person to discuss it. Vincie is a huge supporter of this project, and I'm so glad he agreed to add his creative and artistic touch by doing the cover.

October 2, 2014

Today we cried. All three of us, Winnie, Judy, and I, around the kitchen table as I read.

Even after I warned Winnie and Judy that Chapter 17 was a sad one, even though we all knew it had a happy ending, even though I wrote it and we all knew what was coming next, we still cried imagining how Winnie's family must have felt believing he was dead.

This journey has been filled with lots and lots of laughter and smiles, and now a few tears too. But every good story and every good life has its sad moments...

October 23, 2014

Bittersweet day... last interview. Oh sure, there's lots yet to do and more meetings to have, but today Winnie recounted for me the final interview that will finish the writing of the book.

It's hard to find the words to really describe how I am feeling. I'm so excited to wrap this creation up, to get it published and share Winnie's story with his family and friends, and hopefully even some strangers along the way. As happy as I am for the ending, part of me is sad that this journey is coming to a close.

October 30, 2014

FINISHED!!! Well, almost finished...the writing is done, but there is still some formatting and editing work to do. But, for all intents and purposes, the memoir is pretty much finished.

The closest experience to which I can compare this whole process is having a child. Months of stewing, creating, wondering, laughing, crying, being the last thing I think about before going to sleep and my first thought in the morning. The book...it's always there, exciting and scaring me at the same time. I can't wait to share it with the world, and I want so badly for people to think it's wonderful.

But, truthfully, the people I most want to think it's wonderful do. Winnie and Judy were grinning from ear to ear when I left them after reading the final chapters to them today. Well, grinning through a few more tears... They have bared their souls to me, the details of their personal lives entrusted to my story-telling, and I know this has been an intense, emotional journey for them as well.

I am so very happy… relieved and just a tiny bit sad to turn the page on this part of our adventure. From the very beginning, this book has been a labor of love for all three of us. Only God knows what the next pages will bring…and we entrust the rest of Winnie's story to Him!

Julie and Winnie Nirich, October 2014

The Nirich Family, October 2014

Gary, Judy, Angie, Winnie, and Vinnie

About the Author

photo by Kristoffer Gray

Terry Gray was born and reared in rural Indiana, enjoying an idyllic childhood growing up on the County Line Road with her parents and three younger siblings. Following graduation from Hagerstown High School, Terry pursued her education at Indiana University, earning a Master of Science degree in Elementary Education.

She began dating her future husband, Kim, after she started teaching and coaching at the same country school that she had attended. Little did they know, but their marriage had been "arranged" by their dads long ago, which apparently worked, because in 2015 they will celebrate 35 years of marriage.

Kim and Terry make their home in a country cabin on 35 acres, raising four wonderful children who have flown the nest and have families of their own. They love country life, and unashamedly dote on their six young, beautiful grandchildren.

Terry works part-time as the office administrator for her church, volunteers at the local crisis pregnancy care center, and tries to stay fit by attending YMCA classes and playing tennis a couple of times a week. Her passions are her faith and her family, along with lots of other hobbies including photography, beekeeping, mission work, traveling, and blogging (www.notquitecountrygirl.com). This is Terry's first authored book.

Made in the USA
San Bernardino, CA
03 September 2015